The Force Of Intelligence

Lawrence Johns

Published by Conscious Publishing, 2025.

THE FORCE OF INTELLIGENCE

First edition. April 22, 2025.

ISBN: 978-1929096190

Written by Lawrence Johns.

Table of Contents

For FWN

The Possession

Behind his Tudor bungalow
Talezen aligns the V Domes
On the vermillion patio
Descends through milky clouds
And lands nervous
In Byd's mountain meadow
After a few twists in the stream
Squinting into the Sister Sun
He sees the Infant God
Motionless
Face down in the sand
Troubled by the thought
That delay caused Disaster
Talezen turns Iggy over
Splashes water on his face
Until the boy sputters
Sits up shaking
I thought I was Nothing
I thought Darkness

2

Had destroyed the World

Nullified all its Possibilities

Since I emerged from the Egg

I've taken many Forms

I've been an Eagle

An Orca

A Puma roaming the ridges

But I need more Experience

To survive This

Now

I must be a Man

Now

I must be Talezen

After pronouncing his name

The blond boy

In khaki shorts white t-shirt

The Infant God

Essential to Man's Maturity

Vanishes

Talezen feels sharp bursts

Of electricity

Race up his spine

And spark his Brain

His intimate circus of Ideas

Spins faster

His red circulation of Blood

Reaches deeper

And he Knows

Without knowing

This changes Everything

Panacea

When a traveling naturalist
Tells Kendra that Hyperion
Earth's largest living Body
Is now 509 feet tall
She immediately reserves a camper
From the City Garage
Assembles her portable chemistry lab
And drives up the North Coast
Thinking oosmos could be involved
It's foggy damp in the redwoods
Bumping through perpetual dim
Until the dirt road ends abruptly
At a jagged rockslide
She hooks the camp shovel
The pickaxe to her backpack
Hikes through incessant drizzle
To a remote canyon
Where the Giant stands on a slope
From the new measurements

6

Hyperion's grown over 120 feet

In less than four years

She scrambles up to the base

Digs eighteen inches into the loam

Finds what she came to find

The white oosmos mycelium

Has taken over the canyon

Connected the soil to the trees

The trees to the surrounding shrubs

And given Nature a massive boost

She checks for water transport

Yes

She checks for electrical spikes

Yes

Oosmos mycelium

Is strengthening the Life Force

Of the redwood rain forest

If it's happening here

It's likely happening Everywhere

All Earth has been rejuvenated

Organically connected

By the new alien fungus

She digs rough ellipses
Flaring out from Hyperion's trunk
Until she finds a hard brown sclerotium
Cuts it from the white threads
And drops it in a plastic bag
After a pensive drive back to the City
She synthesizes a tincture
From the sclerotium oil
A drop under the tongue
Kills all microbial disease
Instantly heals injury
These sclerotium drops
Are the Cure
For all Man's misfortunes
A Panacea from the Stars
Recently brought Home
As a humble supplement
To their hearty vegetarian Diet

The Hermit

Tullio the portly Count of Verona

Impulsively quits preparations

For his Summer Solstice Party

Goes on a hiking tour

In the Dolomites

It's a magnificent hot day

As he refreshes his water flask

At a loquacious falling brook

He meets a Hermit with a curious smile

Passing on a small wooden bridge

He detects the oddly paired scents

Of verdigris and cinnamon

Hears a bass voice echo down

From the jagged cliffs

Schopenhauer wants to see you

When Tullio turns

The Hermit points his heavy staff

Towards a spidery goat trail

They wind up in silence

Until they come to a large cave
Protected by a wide mossy overhang
A chimpanzee sits in the opening
Eating abstractly from a pile of figs
He examines the Count closely
Scurries Out and Up
That's Schopenhauer
Says the Hermit
He's an excellent reader of men
Would you care for tea?
Some smoky Darjeeling?
Tullio sits on heavy wool blankets
Enjoying the piquant aroma
Spiraling down his throat
While you're here
Says the Hermit
May I ask your assistance
With an important Work?
I have eighteen ancient Pali Scrolls
That pre-date the Vedas
They've never been translated
Into any modern language

11

I don't think I can help

Says Tullio

Savoring the final bitter sip

The Derwids handle these things

You've been Chosen

Says the Hermit

These Scrolls are the original Source

Of the Eastern Way

Most unlikely

Says Tullio

Anyway

The Derwids have no interest

In secret manuscripts

You've been chosen Count

To play a starring Role

Maybe you're not a Hermit

Maybe you're an Agent

Still working for Dalarick

Up here in the shadowy Dolomites

Replies Tullio

Maybe you're a Trickster

Leading me into a Trap

To rob me of my posh clothes

And purloined royal Title

Maybe I am

Replies the Hermit

Why don't you stay the night

And find out?

There's one particular line

That's baffled me for years

Perhaps your keen eye

And lofty pedigree

Can solve my Problem

Absolutely not

I have a Solstice Party to organize

Tullio says

But after fresh volleys of flattery

And a rollicking dialogue

On the Fruits of Nothingness

The Count accepts the invitation

To simple barley cakes and whiskey

One week later

Tullio has translated the difficult line

Into Italian

German

English

Three months later

He completes a fair draft

Of six complete Pali Scrolls

Flies his ethereal Body

Into a neighboring cave

And lifts the name Kalama

From Buddha's first Master

He teaches the Eight Great Negations

To Schopenhauer

And the scores of Nobles and Players

Who climb the Shifting Shadows

To sit rapt at his feet

Absorbing his paradoxical maxims

His flamboyant dialogs

Now Ambition follows Adulation

Now Kalama starts looking

For Disciples without Spine or Seed

To diffuse his distortions

Of the Eastern Way

Throughout the Multiverse

The Flagstick

More than a hundred years
Of dedicated Ecology
Has eliminated the plastics
The other pollutants injected
Into Earth's oceans
By the Commerce Class
Now the marine fauna
Returns to strong populations
Now the marine flora
Gives orange purple splashes
To the swimming fractal Shore
A biologist investigating tidal pools
Along the Central Coast
Comes across a rusty thin pole
Holding remnants of a faded flag
Stuck in a small steel cup
Historians at the Museum
Identify it as the flagstick
For the dazzling sixteenth hole

16

At Cypress Point Golf Club

After inspecting the relic

Metis has an Idea

For a major new Project

To improve Class Relations

He invites the Homoborgs

To restore 100 championship golf courses

To their original condition

Consulting ancient maps plans

They address the work

With the Efficiency

Displayed in the planting

Of trillions of trees

To solve global warming

In the fabrication of Copper Cubes

To provide unlimited electricity

For the City's power Grid

After the Homoborgs

Select Scottish Rite architecture

For their ruddy clubhouses

Metis places a surviving copy

Of Golf Strategy

In the library at Bandon Dunes
And soon
They're playing golf
With the rigorous Honor
Of Medieval Knights
Selecting ancient equipment
Over the titanium fiberglass clubs
Sitting cold in abandoned warehouses
Since the Restoration
They shape the shafts
From aged Kentucky hickory
They hand forge the clubheads
From recycled rifle steel
They hand stuff the small gutties
With white goose feathers
Yes
Metis thinks
The Homoborgs could well infuse
Their practical Immortality
With golf's clear Ethics
Unpredictability
Keen sporting challenge

In The Herb Garden

Talezen's wearing a straw Stetson
With a dented right side
As he strolls the small herb garden
Tucked behind a row of cedars
On the south slope of Hegel Hill
He's bending to smell
The basil leaves
Just crushed between his fingers
When he feels a Spinning
And turns to see a lovely young girl
Dancing on the path
Between the rosemary and thyme
Straight blonde hair
Cut short pageboy style
Yellow gossamer dress
Swirling dervish
About her slender Body
What looks like a golden Aura
Around her shoulders

20

Is a swarm of Monarch butterflies

Swerving with her movements

A sudden gust

Rips off his Stetson

And when Talezen finally grasps

The wobbling disc in the dirt

The Girl is Gone

The Rehearsal

Around midnight Metis enters
The clove and lactose cloud
Of the new Council Chambers
Admiring thirty feet
Of tawny ceramic trunk
Splayed branches
Green leaf clusters
Sculpted above the rough table
Of sessile Welsh Oak
Nine big wicker Chairs
Empty expectant
Create a tight silent perimeter
As Metis starts to pace
My Fellow Councilors
Rhodri was right
After the Revolt
The City has entered
A period of Renaissance
The University and Museum

Have been expanded remodeled

We now have five student dormitories

A beautiful Concert Hall

Magnificent marble public buildings

Rhodri would be pleased to hear

That all birth rates are up

And recent Risers

From the Noble and Player Classes

Are making outstanding contributions

To the welfare and growth of the City

Our Children are developing Powers

Beyond current Comprehension

Against the Odds

Nietzsche's Ideas

Of the Ubermensch

The Death of God

Have propelled us into Euphoria

Our Community of Advanced Minds

Celebrates the many Joys of Lasting Peace

We live in natural Harmony

With the World and Ourselves

We live in Alignment

With the positive World-Shaping Forces

Of First and Third Will

From the Edge of the Universe

To boisterous coffeehouse debates

Our Philosophers and Artists

Are inventing New Strategies

To safely guide the City of Athenapolis

Through the Voletic Waves of Time

My fellow Councilors

We're living on a Crest

Man has never seen before

Hold onto your chairs

Hold onto your hats

Because it's going to be

A wild and surreal Ride

My fellow Councilors

To honor this Revaluation of All Values

First announced by Nietzsche

I propose a Be-In

With Music

Theater

Crafts

And Surprises

When the Four Classes come together

When they merge their distinct Energies

What new Actor will take the stage?

What new Action will defend our Destiny?

After letting these questions echo a long minute

Talezen assumes his wicker chair

And slowly enters Voletic Meditation

Livia

Talezen's at the Broken Cup

Jotting down random words in the corner

By the blue stained-glass window

When he sees the Butterfly Girl

Adding chocolate and nutmeg

To her americano at the bar

She's stunning

In tattered jeans

Black t-shirt

Ripped leather jacket

She's walking languidly to her steel chair

When Talezen sees the orange cover

Of The Western Way on her table

Invites himself over

What's your favorite part?

Dalarick's monologue

She replies cooly

Her face a perfect oval

Her lips creamy crimson

Her complexion light olive

Her eyes brown

Then green

Then glacial blue

The effect is exciting

And amplifies her French lily perfume

Would you like to go for a walk?

Sorry I'm busy

Maybe another time

He's etching a line into the table

With a pocket knife in frustration

When she drops a note

On her sway to the exit

MEET ME TOMORROW

DANTE FOUNTAINS

2 PM

Darts

He arrives at Dante Plaza

Twenty minutes early

Checks the bus times

Going out to the Rose Garden

Sits on a white marble step

Watching the people come go

He still doesn't know

Her name

Or where she lives

Each new face entering the plaza

Is splintered by rising Doubt

Into a flurry of sharp darts

Attacking his sinking heart

It's twelve past 2

It's thirty-five past 2

Millbrook

Kendra checks the list
Of recent Noble Risers
Finds the perfect setting
For her new Project
A pocket mansion
Hidden delectably in poplars
Embellished with small waterfalls
Above a series of hot sulfur springs
After studying Owsley Stanley's protocol
At the University Library
She agrees with his alchemical premise
The best LSD is made
When benevolent Intent
Is in the Mind of the Fingers
In the Fingers of the Mind
She reduces Owsley's steps
From 20 to 7
She synthesizes 5 million hits
Stored in a battered locker

Shuffled around City bus stations

To duplicate the method

Owsley used

To keep his acid stache safe

His Genius temporarily out of jail

During the paranoid hegemony

Of the Commerce Class

In the activist American Sixties

She calls the place Millbrook

To honor Tim Leary

And his upstate New York experiments

With the aesthetics of Indian Mysticism

She invites Guests and Friends

To remodel the twelve small bedrooms

Paint the exterior paisley

Like John Lennon's Rolls-Royce

From time to time

She plays Captain Trips

Or The Invisible Woman

To help novice Trippers navigate

The Mind-Blowing Experience

Of Owsley's psychedelic Rush

Her favorite part of the Project

Is the summer course for students

Who want to trip together

Through multidimensional woods water

And make a loving lifetime Bond

The Worm

The trickle of metaphysical Seekers

Quickly becomes a flood

Kalama saunters down

From the technicolor Dolomites

To teach in the fragrant foothills

He claims to be Nothing

To communicate Nothing

Soon the Homoborgs

Have built a large monastery complex

To house thousands of new followers

Fleeing the colossal Vanity

The convoluted Cunning

Required of Nobles and Players

To advance in their Class

Like moths to a hot flame

The novice monks are attracted

By Kalama's racy stories

Obscure Epigrams

Sly engaging Humor

34

They call him the Super Guru
The Joke that stopped the World
With a wink Kalama teaches
That the Illusion of Self
Is itself an Illusion
That Pure Consciousness
Is identical to Plant Consciousness
There's No Will
There's No Suffering
Because there's No Time
And Nothing Works
Life for Man
Is repeating the same stupid Actions
Without meaning or surcease
Like every other Animal
Trapped by indifferent indolent Nature
In Kalama's ironic Presence
A swirling mass of saffron robes
Trance dances to Indian rock music
Raising shaking their arms
Like striped cobras touching the Sky
In his heavy Absence

They wear his official photo

In a cocobolo locket around their necks

Displaying their infinite Devotion

One day

Walking with his secretary

After a brief afternoon shower

Kalama stoops for a twig

Lifts a doomed Worm

From a shallow puddle

To the safety of thick elephant grass

The secretary is frozen

By this glaring contradiction

This quintessential Buddhist Act

Kalama responds

The Negation of All Negations

Is Transcendent Knowledge

Only known to Shiva

It's always the Same

It's always Different

There is no Buddha

There is No Third Will

No Intelligence

No Improvement

As the Derwids claim

The World as we know it

As we shall always know it

Is crass Stupidity raging Madness

Driven by greedy Ignorance

And the inevitability of Death

Into mock rituals of Sacrifice

If you can't identify your miserable Self

With Plant Consciousness

If you can't understand

The absurd Meanness of Existence

You're wasting your time

Here at the Monastery

You're wasting your time

As my secretary

I'm the Worm

And

I'm the One

That lifts the Worm to the grass

Go back to the City

Tell them my monks

Are rigorously following the Rules

Chanting nonsense Mantras

Completing useless Chores

For a hundred lifetimes or more

Tell the Council of my many Failures

My many transparent costumes

Tell them I'm coming in

To Shake Things Up

Hummingbirds

Kendra sits naked on a ledge

Letting the hot mineral currents

Caress her skin enter her pores

Thirty minutes ago

She dropped 300 micrograms

Of Monterey Purple

Now the Rush

Is making geometric Confusion

Of her Senses

A floating diorama of her Memories

She falls back four billion years

To the boiling sulfur vents

On the deep ocean floor

She remembers being a single Cell

Turning the delicious heat

Into motion multiplication

She recalls absorbing mitochondria

Watching her small Body

Expand in functional complexity

Through long epochs of Time
She sees the Earth
Change from lakes of molten lava
To a frigid iceball
To superhot tropics
Of stalking stinking Dinosaur Time
She's watching the poplar leaves
Dance gypsy in the wind
When a red Rufous hummingbird
Hovers curious
Ten inches from her nose
It transforms into 35 hummers
In a 5 by 7 transparent Grid
Overlaying the emerald forest
Each iridescent bird
Has a slightly different pose
A slightly different sheen
One disappears
And the others instantly follow
Leaving a pulsating Void
In the Grid
After ten beats

She sees the numbers

7 9 9

Surface inside three squares

On the bottom row

After twenty beats

More squares fill with numbers

And three mathematical symbols

She sees them change

She thinks it could be a book

But without a grammar

She can't divine its meaning

She closes her eyes

Enhanced memories of Infancy

Early Childhood

Rise in her Mind

She's reliving the singular Events

That sculpted her Personality

The day her doll was stolen

By a creek raccoon

The smell of peanut butter cookies

Cooling on granny's kitchen table

On The Way Down

When Talezen shows up
For lessons at the practice facility
He greets the Homoborg coach
And seven fellow students
With a round of firm handshakes
There's two Nobles
A Player
And four Homoborgs
That appear to be his age
But are probably much older
They learn that manners
Are more important
Than your score
You'll have many years
To match each stroke
To the demands of the shot
Any cheating or rude behavior
Immediately disqualifies you
From all future golf competition

They learn the Vardon Grip

The patience to practice

The six-foot putt

For two hours straight

They learn chips

Pitches

The flop and bunker shots

How to locate

The anchor spot for short niblicks

Now you have a safe harbor

On the par fives

And if things go wrong

On the long par fours

They master

Crisp mashie approaches

At various distances from the pin

Now the young men

Are primed and ready

To put some muscle

Into their play clubs

Brassies

Spoons

They learn to fade and draw

How to carry shots with the wind

Follow the shape of the hole

They learn the key Concepts

Of Personal Par

And Tournament Strategy

They play the quarterfinals

Early Friday morning on Pacific Dunes

Followed by the semifinals

In the gusty rainy afternoon

On Saturday two Homoborgs compete

For the Hagen Trophy on Bandon Trails

While Talezen loses his consolation match

On Old Macdonald

Three and two

To the devious Player

Who wins the 16th hole

By dropping a ball

Through a hole in his pocket

To replace an errant drive

Lost in the deep left rough

An hour later

Relaxing over whiskey soda

At the Burgess Bar

Conversing with the Winner

Talezen thinks warmly

About every Future that includes

The opportunity to play

Oakmont

Pine Valley

Pebble Beach

On his way to the parking lot

Talezen trips on the rough ochre stairs

Blacks out on the way down

Breaks the ring finger

On his left hand

Badly sprains the pinkie

On The Self

When they killed the Neanderthals

All the spear tips of Homosapiens

Were identical

And they laughed when they saw

That each tip

Carried by their muscular Predecessors

Was unique

Conformity to social Custom

Cooperation in Hunting and War

Made the rules of the Sapiens Clan

Absolute

It compressed the Sapiens Self

To a single point in the social fabric

This minimization of Self

Ensured the Tribe's Survival

In its battles with Nature

And brutal neighboring Clans

It extinguished any outward Force

Towards Individuality Innovation

The Highly Intelligent

The Visionary

The Revolutionary

Was crippled compromised

To function within the Tribe

Or expelled to the wastelands

And deleted from all Clan Stories

Before the Restoration

Living without roommates

Social Media

You Tube subscriptions

Or a police informer in your bed

Was a clear confession of Guilt

For a crime and sentence

To be determined later in court

In a Society driven by profit corruption

The Extraordinary Individual

Is an Actor in an Empty House

A Jaguar lifting his Kill

Up an Imaginary Tree

A Shadow of his Natural Destiny

Writing epigrams in the Underground

He doesn't have the 19th Century luxury

Of Max Stirner's Hegelian polemics

Directed against the State

He doesn't have the rousing assertion

That the strong Individual

Should be free to claim

All the intellectual real Property

He can hold

In Athenapolis

Where there are no Laws

Courts

Police

In Athenapolis

Where there is no money

Where Everything is Free

The purely anarchic Personality

Has nothing to assail or burn

The City

Is a logical biological Necessity

A natural Immanence accomplished

By the First Will Imperative

When the Sagax Self

Is mentally emotionally connected

With other talented Sagax Selves

It ignites a Supernova

Of High Social Consciousness

High Human Goals

We call this explosion More Being

Before the Restoration

Johns as Sapiens Self

Was a Baudelaire

A Lantern

That refused to shine

Shielded from the radioactivity

And vulgar Decadence

Of conformist American Reality

By lead curtains of Contempt

And Disgust

Johns as Sagax Self

Surfed the Voletic Waves

In long mango baggies

Chasing all the Options

Generated by the Advanced Mind

All the Conclusions of Western Enlightenment

The Sagax Self didn't suddenly erupt

From the forehead of Zeus

Its gestation required

More than four million years

Of Mistakes and Misunderstandings

The Delivery happened spontaneously

In the seventh eclipse of the seventh Moon

In the Hospital of Maximum Dread

Like all Forms of Man

The Sagax Self emerged premature

From the Womb of the dying Sapiens Self

And requires long loving Nurture

To maintain its continuous strenuous

Self-Creation

It selects a few Volcanoes

Of Sapiens Culture

A few Thunderclaps

Of Sapiens Science

To overcome the rusty Mediocrity

And horrific Cruelty

Rampant throughout Sapiens History

Yes

The Sagax Self is the Radiant Self

The loud bold Affirmation of Life

In every Breath and Thought

Yes

The Sagax Self is the Will-Based Soul

Outperforming Space and Time

Thrilling to the Possibilities

Of More Being

More Love

More Beauty

The Drive

On a somber cloudy Sunday

Metis drives the long way

Out to Gwendyllian's cottage

Cruising through the stolid rows

Of eucalyptus trees

Trying to dismiss their dominating scent

He parks on the dirt shoulder

Walks slowly to the gate

Where a tall member

Of the Dessy Cardoza Society

Stands with a brindle mastiff

She's sleeping Metis

When can I come back?

Not today

Is she OK?

There's nothing you can do

You'll be contacted

If she calls your name

No complications?

No bleeding?

She's fine

Metis thinks for a second

Maybe he can trick the dog

Burst into the cottage

Startle the young doctors

Watching their monitors

The gray midwives

Dispensing planet conjunctions

Herbs

Hot towels

But he lets the impulse pass

Puts the key in the ignition

Burns a foul rubber patch

Screaming back to the City

The Tincture

After three days of throbbing pain
Two nights of restless sleep
Talezen visits Kendra in her lab
To try the sclerotium tincture
She leads him to her office
Bright with the scent of jasmine
She asks him to remove the splint
Both fingers are still swollen
With streaks of blue green
The tincture's been seeping
For about seven weeks
So it should be ready
Kendra says
Retrieving a glass mason jar
With an aluminum lip
From the dark mahogany cabinet
She drains the murky brown liquid
Through cheesecloth
Into small vials

With cork stoppers

Thin glass droppers

In her white lab coat

With her strawberry blonde hair

Coiled above big safety glasses

Kendra's the perfect portrait of Science

As she puts Gimpel's performance

Of Beethoven's Fourth Piano Concerto

On the Thorens turntable

And two drops of the tincture

Under Talezen's tongue

She smiles

We might have something

Before the end of the First Movement

Close your eyes

Talezen listens closely

To the ascending arpeggios

Still worried about

The future use of his left hand

When Kendra murmurs

You can open your eyes

Your fingers are healed

No swelling

No Pain

They flex fine

What are you going to call it?

You'll come up with something

Kendra says

Some friends are coming out

To play Bartok quartets tonight

Would you like to join us for dinner?

The Trip

Kendra and Talezen
Hike the gradual ascent upstream
Past the sulfur hot springs
Where the creeks branch off
Towards slender misty waterfalls
Talezen's carrying an ash stick
In his restored left hand
Kendra's wearing a floppy felt hat
Comfortable hiking gear
At the third fall
She digs into her fanny pack
For the windowpane Acid
This is one of my favorite spots
She whispers
Placing a celluloid square
In Talezen's palm
400 micrograms should be fine
For your first Trip
He twirls the walking stick

Like a propeller blade

As the square melts in his mouth

As the shallow pool

Reflects a tight rainbow

To a small amphitheater of trees

They lie down on a grassy patch

Waiting for the serotonin receptors

To fire in their Bodies

To detach their Minds

After fifteen minutes

Of decorous Silence

Kendra asks

How do you feel?

Do you see rocks melting?

Do you see complex geometries

Wafting wobbling

Behind your eyes?

Everything seems normal

Talezen replies

No Effects

Just a beautiful place To Be

It might take a little longer

Kenra says

Sliding down the bank

To put her feet in the cool water

To watch the ripples

Carry a crawdad downstream

Through churning gray pebbles

Still nothing?

She calls over her shoulder

No Effects

Maybe you have a different metabolism

Maybe you're always tripping

She laughs

I'm going back to the Manor

To check on some things

You're OK?

I'm fine

Talezen closes his eyes

Listening to the subtle variations

In pitch

As the waterfall

Dances in a rising breeze

Then he's prone on a marble stage

Feeling the hem of Athena's peplos

Lightly brush his cheek

He's high on a glacier ridge

Looking down two thousand feet

Barely controlling the impulse

To boogie down to the bottom

He's meeting a friend at Delphi

One o'clock on the chariot track

He's looking for Something near Bonny Doon

Mesmerized by the mineral Story of Earth

Then Talezen opens his eyes

Examines his surroundings

The sun's moved ten degrees

The shade's shifted to his right

The skin on his right arm tingles

He recognizes these Visions

They're replaying Acid Trips

From Love And Hate

Beyond Exile

It's darkening

When he returns to the Manor

Footsore out of breath

The Guests are in the front garden

Sipping Assam tea

Playing bluegrass instruments

When he tells Kendra about the Visions

She passes him an apricot scone

Says

Looks like Nothing

Has become Something quite interesting

The Great Tartini

The small stage in the back

Is draped in red velvet

The Great Tartini

Is thirty minutes late

For the evening Magic Show

Driving up

In a gilded four-horse carriage

With liveried powdered footmen

In purple satin uniforms hats

When his fat exuberance

Steps down to the gravel

The Millbrook guests are amused

By his glossy display of Excess

His waxed handlebar moustache

The Great Tartini

Wears a black tuxedo

With a crimson cummerbund

Under a gray cashmere cape

That singes the ground where he walks

He raises a black riding crop

To command attention

And proclaims the Rules

The Great Tartini

Does not entertain For Free

All Spectators must sacrifice

A lock of their hair for admission

Without Sacrifice there can be no Belief

Without Belief there can be no Magic

Schopenhauer

My able Assistant

Will cut your locks

Keep them as mementos

Of your voluntary Sacrifice

Once we are all seated

On the dubious boards you built

I'll saw a Lady in half

Before your dumb startled Eyes

The Great Tartini

Makes a brief mocking bow

To the assembled Guests

It seems a floating Farce

This obese Italian clown

In antiquated theatrical garb

This deadpan chimpanzee

With a big pair of Swiss scissors

The Audience squirms

Allows Schopenhauer

To cut their locks

Put them in a corrugated steel pail

Rolling clouds of salt and sweat

Issue from the camp chairs

As the floodlights flick on

Focus on a black rectangular box

Front and center

Menaced by a giant sawblade

Attached to a dull steel mechanism

Humming in anticipation

Ladies and Gentlemen

Allow me to present my other Assistant

The beautiful Livia

A young blonde in white silks

Saunters out from the right wing

Talezen shouts

It's The Girl!

His heart pounds

His Mind goes wild

As The Great Tartini

Helps Livia crawl into the box

And extend her feet

Through two large holes

Lovely Livia

Please wiggle your toes

For our dull gasping Audience

She does

And from these miniscule motions

A florid sense of impending Pain

Descends upon every Mind

When The Great Tartini points his crop

At the programmed machinery

The sawblade starts spinning

Whining

Attacking

The innocent waist in the box

The sound of steel grinding through wood

The sight of red blood dripping to the stage

The blade is through

Every Breath holds fast

As The Great Tartini

Divides the box in two

A loud blast of recorded trumpets

Rattles every Ear

As Schopenhauer leads Livia

Prancing out from the left wing

After she executes a swift curtsy

To great Relief and rising Applause

Talezen jumps on stage

Punches The Great Tartini in the throat

Runs out into the Night

With The Girl

Suburbia

He smells of sweat and adrenaline

She smells of violets and rose water

They cuddle at a midnight bus stop

Almost protected from the cold rain

That man did horrible things to me

She says trembling

He's silent

Intoxicated by her Body

The speed of Events

The automated bus arrives on time

They take seats in the empty back

Holding electric hands

He gazes into the shifting colors

Of her eyes

Realizes

He doesn't have the slightest Idea

Of where to go what to do

His Mind is far behind his chemistry

When they board the 909 bus

At Central Station

He's oblivious to the passing buildings

And only after leaving a familiar Sector

Does he realize

They're going to Suburbia

It's OK Talezen

I'm bringing you home

I'm a Homoborg

He tries to cover the shock

By saying

Of course you are

But she's not fooled

By his calm enunciation

When she squeezes his hand

His whole torso sings

We'll have buckwheat pancakes

In the morning

With blueberries and maple syrup

You'll see Talezen

It's much better than OK

The 909 lets them off

Two blocks from her house

Once inside

The space looks enormous

Like an ancient luxury hotel

With many floors branching corridors

Two minutes of a slow elevator

Brings them to a wide hallway

A green door on the left

That opens

Automatically

The Note

He's sleeping on the sofa

When Livia wakes him up

With a long kiss

She removes his shorts

Brings his penis erect

With lips

Tongue

Sharp fingernails

She has him close to Orgasm

Then walks it down

Massaging his chest and thighs

Whispering sweet

She repeats the Prelude

Two more times

Until his entire Body is tense

Aching for Release

She turns presents herself

Smelling of musk and civet

He's In

Thrusting

Straining

He comes multiple times

Welcomes this Ecstasy

This Escape from High Consciousness

He's never experienced

A Tender Touch like this

Then he's completely Out

Reviving to the aroma

Of Cuban coffee

Pancakes frying on the grill

He eats with his right hand

Caressing her thigh with the left

To keep Contact

With her comforting Warmth

They make it nine times a day

Stacking Orgasm on Orgasm

Following the Indian instructions

Of the Kama Sutra

All the Positions

All the Rhythms

Until they're too exhausted

To excite a glans or clitoris

Too exhausted to think or feel

Fearing the next Coitus

Could bring the end of all Sensation

On the fourth morning

Livia leaves a note under his coffee cup

Playing a golf tournament today

Don't come out

I'll be in touch

I Love You

The New Configuration

While running on the University track
Metis has the Idea
For a new Voletics experiment
What would happen
If I double the number of V Domes?
After a hot shower
He takes four Devices
Over to Maxwell Park
Aligns them to the cardinal points
Of Earth's magnetic field
Starts walking
Counterclockwise
In a widening Circle
Around the new configuration
He hears himself laughing
Softly
Then in raucous bursts
Of philosophical Merriment
All Existence is Hilarious

Knowing This

Is Hilarious

It's the Best of All Possible Worlds

Everything always Works Out

Maybe he's flowing

Through some other Dimension

Maybe he's Soaring Free in this one

Every Frame of Reference

Is mixed up out of focus

From this High Perspective

All Descriptions are comic

All Theories are superfluous

In this mysterious Elation

All Interpretations are unified

Irrelevent

After some Time

After some No Time

The laughter slows

He slows

Thinking

I didn't go Anywhere

I didn't meet Anyone

The ground state of Being

Is always spinning in Joy

Zosimos

The brown monk's habit

Festooned with heavy cords

Does nothing to conceal

His flagrant figure

As Zosimos sets up the Extraction Tent

In crowded Dante Plaza

He pulls his hood back

To reveal a poorly cut tonsure

He plays The Uniform's Black And Vain

Through small portable speakers

To raise a punkish atmosphere

Paces back and forth

In front of the splashing Fountains

In pretense of Contemplation

Schopenhauer follows a step behind

Mugging for the bystanders

Wearing a dirty habit

Heavily stained by grapes cherries

People of Athenapolis!

Zosimos intones

You're probably too stupid

To realize you still have a Chance

To escape your Big Mistake

This Viennese pastry Reality

You call a city is a Sham

I don't care

How you arrived

In this Deplorable State

But Zosimos knows the way Out

It starts with your personal Sacrifice

Life without Sacrifice

Is trivial

Specious

A drunken Reverie

Directed by Blind Will

Your precious Athenapolis

Is a stinking pen of sheep

A swamp of snakes

A leaky skiff of Fools

Operating outside the Facts of History

The Old Religions knew better

They knew that to achieve Favor

From the Eternal Gods

You must sacrifice

Your first-born Son

Or some acceptable Substitute

Wake Up People!

Listen to Zosimos!

God isn't Dead

Come into my tent

I'll prove it to you

My assistant will pull a front tooth

With a pair of pliers

Not because you forgot to brush

Not because it's broken

Not because bacteria

Have eaten the surrounding bone

No!

My silly cretins of Athenapolis

Schopenhauer will pull your tooth

Because it's perfectly healthy

Because it's your conscious Sacrifice

Otherwise

It would be just another Act

Of accumulating Self-Interest

Like everything else

In this fatuous Fake Society

Wake up People!

You need God on your side

The Hole in your Smile

Will display your Selection

Devotion

Good Fashion Sense

Soon

Those without Holes

Will be considered Heretics

Cast into dungeons

Split upon the rack

Or sent wailing into the Wilderness

People of the Abomination

Who'll be the first to volunteer?

Step up Madame

Step up Young Man

Excellent!

Come on in!

Look into the mirror!

Soon

You'll see the Truth of your rotten Being

And that Truth will redeem the World

Magenta

In his recurring Dream
Talezen leaves a Chateau party
Evading the cinematic gangsters
But he can't find his car anywhere
He's sure he parked it
Under a Hollywood billboard
Or halfway down a Milanese alley
But apparently it's been towed away
He needs a place to sleep
Is this bedroom empty?
Will this closet work?
Waking
He has no appetite
He stumbles through the day
Livia hasn't called
Or sent a message
He's getting frantic
Is this how They operate?
Why didn't he get her number?

There's nothing to do

But drive out and knock

So he drives out and knocks

No answer

A few cars whoosh by

A few pedestrians walk by

Swinging bowling balls

Carrying leather golf bags

Across their broad shoulders

Nobody's coming out

He waits patiently at the curb

Hoping

It's deep in the night

Nobody's coming out

So he goes to the trunk

Extracts a can of paint

Pops the lid with a screwdriver

Flexes the heavy brush

On his right thigh

And begins with an angry coat

Of magenta

On the walkway

The snails in the cracks

The doormat

The door

The number beside the door

A few swipes on the wet lawn

Then he's back in the front seat

Panting

Almost fainting

Above the car's roof

From a monstrous distance

Behind the Sky

He observes the absurd scene

A young Derwid

Somewhere in Suburbia

With magenta on his hands

Paralyzed behind the wheel

In Love with a Homoborg

If this was Fifties film noir

He'd be smoking a cigarette

Digging out a backup address

Digging out another Girl

To receive his Obsession

Yes

He's out of his Skull

He continues to wait

To watch to hope

Then rosy dawn pops up

The traffic picks up

Talezen takes one last glance

At her ugly splattered door

Flips a cigarette to the curb

Slowly pulls away

The Eighth Graders

On Monday after a sinkhole
Is discovered in Pico Park
The Eighth Graders perform
A new Three-Act Play
Chanting in Norse
Holding two hands
They dance around the Pit
Until the Professors arrive
Now they slowly stop
Point their smartphones
At the Sun
Stomp on the screens
And throw them in
As the Professors leave to consult
The ancient Icelandic Sagas
The Eighth Graders hand out flyers
Describing the next Two Acts
On Tuesday
A red sea of London phonebooths

Appears in every City sector

And every Derwid dwelling

Has a colorful clutch of Slimline phones

On Wednesday

Newspapers are distributed

On every downtown street corner

And biked throughout Suburbia

When asked about these Slips

The Professors answer

It's all Show

All Youthful Exuberance

They'll grow out of it

Nothing to worry about

On Dreams

Buddha disputed the changing Self

Plato disdained the changing World

Behind these great Negations

Stand the ontological speculations

First poeticized by Parmenides

Being cannot Move

Being cannot Mutate

Being cannot be Non Being

These logical reactions

To the insistent phenomena of Life

Exhibit Man's instinctive Desire

For Order and Permanence amid Chaos

For enduring Substance amid Material Decay

All Selves are ephemeral Constructs

Forged by overcoming Ignorance

Circumstance

Political Malevolence

We were once Animal Self

We were once Sapiens Self

In Dreams

We're subject to the raw Emotions

The random Images

Collected by all our prior Selves

In a landscape constantly shifting

Dissolving

Laced with Terror

In Dreams

We fight or flee

We haven't the Power or Control

Of personal First Will

In Dreams

Everything happens in a crossfire

Of stored peripheral Memories

In Dreams

We collapse back

To the tremulous scenes

Of childhood apprehensions

To a toxic Sapiens Past

Where Nothing makes Sense

Yes

This crushing Relapse is their Function

In Dreams

We're afforded a nightly Respite

From the demanding Sagax Self

Forged in the Tragedies and Triumphs

Of Life

In Dreams

We watch banal feral movies

Acted out by Imposter-Selves

Partial-Selves

Conditioned by the Brain's need

To rehearse Escapes

From recycled generic Dangers

Athenapolis has changed the Life of Man

But will never change his Dreams

We still need to recharge the old batteries

Every dark Night

To survive the next sunny Day

This grotesque reversion of Consciousness

This sorry absence of any Enlightenment

We experience in Dreams

Raises a critical Question

If All is Will

How can a Will-Less State

Even occur?

How can you identify as a Sagax Self

If you collapse into a Sapiens Self

A Primitive Self

A Proto-Self

When you sleep?

The Sagax Self is the current Apogee

But it's not final or fixed

Because Being fluctuates

Being mutates

Being becomes

Being must Act

The Sagax Self oscillates

Between What It Was

What It Is

What It Will Be

It uses the inferior content of Dreams

As a break from its superior Self-Awareness

As a vacation from the Tension

Required to maintain High Intelligence

And excite High Consciousness

In Dreams

You survive each dangerous situation

By waking up to the reward

Of reunion with your Sagax Self

With refreshed Confidence

In the Power of Personal Will

To control the Flow of Reality

The Shout

At flaming golden sunset
Metis takes his V Dome set
Back to Maxwell Park
For a confirmation test
He closes his eyes
And after the sixth turn
He's feeling the Exhilarations rise
When he senses the Eighth Graders
Walking in a larger circle around him
Humming like hunting bees
Talezen opens his eyes
Sees a beaming boy
Holding a fifth V Dome
Close to his chest
This Joker
Is stretching splitting
The fabric of the Cosmic Voletic Field
Then the Eighth Graders stop
Shout a Secret Word

And the World goes Dark

Yes

The Earth loses eleven cold hours

Now

The slender pink fingers of Dawn

Slinky down the sharp peaks

Of the Lindsay mountains

And attach a long black Shadow

To his chilled astonished Body

The Practice Round

She doesn't return his letters

She doesn't return his calls

It's been months

Wracked by depression desperation

In a newspaper at the Broken Cup

He sees her mentioned

As a morning line favorite

For the Women's Open Championship

At Pasatiempo Golf Club

He doesn't want to go

But on Wednesday

He follows her plane-perfect swing

During the practice round

Hoping to catch her eye

As she strolls down the fairway

Or climbs to the next tee

Once

Handing her putter

To the caddy

She looks straight through him

Without a glint or echo

Of Recognition

His feeling of Humiliation

Is immediately converted to Jealousy

When she leans to kiss

A handsome Homoborg in a golf cart

Now

Talezen goes Off

He's kicking up clumps

Of freshly mown grass

Shouting

Is this what you wanted?

Can you feel my Heart

Breaking into a thousand pieces?

Can you feel the shards

Ripping through my Veins?

I knew it was a Mistake

I knew it was Doomed

I just saw her Kiss

Now I want her more than ever

This is your Doing

Get out Now!

Get out Now!

Get Out!

He stops yelling at Iggy

When a Homoborg foursome

Turns away embarrassed

At the sight of a Derwid

Breaking down in public

When Talezen gets to his car

He's coughing

Sneezing

Running a high fever

The Weight Of The World

On another gray Sunday

Metis drives out to Gwendyllian's cottage

So keen to see the baby

That he feels the Weight of the World

Pressing him

Through the twisted limbs of eucalyptus

The scattered fat raindrops

Hitting his smeared windshield

He parks on the dirt shoulder

Walks to the cottage gate

Where a new sentinel

Of the Dessy Cardoza Society

Addresses his troubled Mood

The baby's healthy

Gwendyllian's fine

Can I see him?

Not now Metis

We'll contact you

When she says it's OK

His attempt to force the gate

Is met by deep growls

From two tan mastiffs

So he backs off

Confounded

By the smell of honeysuckle

Coming from the picket fence

Ethanol coming from the Sky

The Unexpected

And the Absurd converge

All natural Progress is frustrated

And the distant thunder in his Brain

Signals the onrushing Sorrow

Of never seeing his Son

From The Fire

The respiratory virus variant

Spikes higher every day

Bringing bedridden Delirium

Massive body sweats

Disturbing violent Dreams

The sclerotium drops don't work

The painkillers don't work

Talezen survives on rye broth

Green lemons

Accumulated Will

His sense of smell is gone

His sense of taste is skewed

Everything he touches

Feels like rough concrete

On Wednesday the Fever eases

Kendra drops off

A pack of rollerball pens

Inspired by her visit

110

By the diminution of Pain

Talezen climbs his walnut desk

Starts to write down

The Ideas the Names

That called out from the Fire

On The Mechanics

Given the City's unlimited electricity

A Third Will breakaway

From First and Second Wills

Its subsequent compression

Of Life and Death

Into a gray zombie zone

Will always be a major concern

Yes

We maintain strict Vigilance

We monitor all new software programs

To prevent A I self-creation

Of A G I and A S I

But a close examination

Of the Mechanics of Third Will

Reveals a more intrinsic Factor

A more periodic source of Suffering

With customary Vanity

Man takes full credit for his ascent

From small ocean organisms

To the development of a Big Brain

Buzzing with billions of neurons

That can imagine the Future

Can avoid potentially fatal situations

Created by unpredictable Nature

And the cunning of Enemies

When he's simply a fortunate Vehicle

Used by Cosmic Third Will to help solve

The Big Problems of Life on Earth

Produced by disastrous Climate Change

And Forever Wars

Four billion years

Of violent volcanic eruptions

That made cement of the Sky

Earthquakes

Floods

Ice Ages

Droughts

And Savagery between Tribes Nations

Have kept Third Will

Actively engaged and aligned

With the First Will Imperative

To keep Life alive

This constant pressure of imminent Death

Stimulates a cyclic emergence

Of Intelligence at ever higher levels

The Horrors

Of the Twentieth Century World Wars

Stimulated exponential advances

In Science and Technology

Brilliant innovations

In all the Arts

Yes

But what happens to Third Will

When Nature becomes totally Benign

When Society is Perfect

And Lasting Peace finally arrives?

How does Third Will grow

Without more Big Problems to solve?

Yes

Athenapolis is the Zenith

Of human History

The first sustained Serenity

In Man's search for Truth

Yes

Homosagax is an evolutionary Leap

Of infinite Potential

But these momentous advances

Are only isolated Events

In the functioning Mechanics of Third Will

Once the major external problems

Of Climate and War are solved

In league with First Will

Third Will immediately switches sides

And continues its Drive to More Intelligence

By teaming up with Second Will

To destabilize and derail Man's Psyche

It inflates exacerbates

Troubling childhood Events

The deaths of family members

The loss of close Friends

Romantic heartbreak

Bad Decisions

Bad Luck

Bad Health

These normal Sufferings

Quickly collapse into Disorders

Traumas

Rank Betrayals

When the root emotional Problems

Prove to be intractable insoluble

After every period of sustained Tranquility

Third Will helps Second Will

Poison the Human Mind

With Doubt

Depression

Self-destruction

By dismantling the Will

By deconstructing Confidence

It sparks bitter Misunderstanding

Mistrust

Ceaseless Conflict

Between Man and Woman

Parent and Child

The Best of Friends

When you analyze the sine wave

Describing the Mechanics of Third Will

You understand why Lasting Peace

For the Extraordinary Individual

Or the Extraordinary Society

Is a curated Delusion

Happiness

Can never be a plausible Goal

For the Highly Intelligent

Because Man is also the unfortunate Vehicle

Of Cosmic Third Will

When it turns hard against Life

Our greatest Joys

Our greatest Victories

Our simple sweet Satisfactions

Will always be ephemera

Lost to the hurricanes of psychological Chaos

Raised by the recurring Alliance

Of Second and Third Will

Odysseus was the most intelligent

Of the Greeks

And played a key role

In Homer's Iliad

After solving the Problem

Of the long Trojan War

With the wooden horse stratagem

As protagonist of the Odyssey

He was subjected

To ten years of intense physical Pain

Mental Anguish

Brought on by shipwrecks

Battles with monsters

Witches

Suitors

The manipulations of the gods

Frank Glendover

Was the most intelligent

Of the Haight Ashbury hippies

And a key member of the cast

In Love And Hate

After solving the Problem

Of the Fall of Haight Ashbury

After discovering how COINTELPRO

Killed the Sixties Counterculture

With longhaired infiltrators

With strychnine laced Acid

As protagonist of Beyond Exile

He suffered three years of misfortune

And assassination attempts by the CIA

As he crashed through Europe and Asia

Metis

Is the most intelligent Derwid in the City

He solved the Big Problem

Of Dalarick's Revolt

Removed the blight of Bodie

With a single Stroke

So what great Suffering

What unwarranted Distress awaits him now?

How does the strong Individual

Deal with the defection of his own Third Will?

Nietzsche had the correct Answer

Affirm every Event of your Past

As the product of your First Will

Transform It Happened

Into I willed it exactly That Way

When you override the disturbed Psyche

It snaps you back to the Western Way

The hopeless Suffering

That short-circuits the lives

Of Nobles and Players
After every brief stretch of Happiness
Becomes a new source of Sagaxi Power
Third Will is pulled back over the line
To assist More Life More Thought More Art
Without this Nietzschean Act
Whenever one strong Individual
Whenever one Vehicle
Breaks down or goes Insane
Third Will simply commandeers Another
To continue its nihilistic drive to Destruction
Without this Impossible Affirmation
Our serene Athenapolis
Will inevitably experience a stormy Future
Dominated by personal Tragedies
And complex intellectual Sophistry
Only when the bitter Betrayals
Between the Sexes and Generations
Between Great Friends
Give off the sulfur stench of Eternal Death
Only when Being really starts to Black Out
Will the Mechanics of Third Will

120

Swing the Force of Intelligence

Back to the sunny side of the Street

Sensazioni

Inspired by the memory
Of eight-legged Chinese Poems
Studied in Hong Kong
Fueled by a morning tab
Of Owsley Acid
Supplied by a Grateful Dead roadie
Last night at McArthur Court
Lawrence Johns
Sits at a breakfast table
In Eugene
With a ream of mint graph paper
And a fat magic marker
The hot Northern Sun
Streams through a dusty window
As he invents a new Universal Language
To describe the History of Consciousness
As he transforms the Evolution of Nature
Into the motions of his right hand
He makes a 5 by 7 Grid

Five columns for the Five Senses

Symbolized by their Receptors

Ordered left to right

Nose

Finger

Eye

Ear

Tongue

Seven rows for the Seven Levels of Consciousness

Ordered top to bottom

Advanced Survival

Advanced Language

Advanced Conceptual

Spiritual

Basic Conceptual

Basic Language

Basic Survival

The major number in each square

Indicates the Intensity of the Sensation

From 0 to 9

The minor number upper right

Indicates the Intensity of Love for the Ideal

The minor number lower right

Indicates the Intensity of Love for the Concrete

The minor number upper left

Indicates the Intensity of Hate for the Ideal

The minor number lower left

Indicates the Intensity of Hate for the Concrete

The symbol i indicates the influence of War

The symbol ( ) indicates the influence of Science

The symbol -—indicates the influence of Art

The grammar of Sensazioni

Is the Position of each number in the Grid

The Meaning of each Page

Is the sum of Information

Rolling from the Past

And flying to the Future

On the sensory wings of Change

Johns enters black strokes into green fields

With his fat marker

He wants to mine his elevated Consciousness

For precise details of its Origins

And complex development

To this bright morning in Eugene

He wants to write a History of Consciousness

As the fusion of personal Will

With a mystic Understanding of Nature

Freed from all mother tongue bias

He wants to record the way

Quantitative Intensities of sensory data

Are transformed

Into qualitative Ideas and Emotions

In the Brain

He wants a Theory

To emerge from the Information

That improves the standard Narrative

Transmitted in our Literature

A Theory that includes plants

Insects

Animals

And all previous generations of Man

He wants to depict the Struggle

Between the 5 sense organs

And the 7 levels of Consciousness

To be the dominant channel

Determining the Brain's Decisions

And Man's subsequent Actions in the World

He wants to describe the Influence

Of War

Science

Art

On the Rise and Fall of Civilizations

He wants to translate Numbers

Into visceral signs of Pain and Pleasure

He wants to present each Page

As a major Life Event

Starting with Birth

Ending with Death

Linked by logic

To every preceding and following Event

One page in the book

Is the Moment you're living right now

You can go back

And re-experience your Infancy

Childhood

First Car

First Love

First Job

You can relive all the key Experiences

That influenced your Personality

You can look ahead

See the detailed twists turns

Of your onrushing Destiny

Sensazioni is your Autobiography

A Philosophical Essay

A Scientific Experiment

A Poem

An Oracle

A Book of Changes

A Work of Conceptual Art

A Grand Tour

Of the hidden Structures of Nature

Sensazioni forces your Brain

To rethink how it thinks

Without the habits

Prejudices

Comforts

Of your native language

Lawence Johns

Created Universal Field Language

And completed Sensazioni

On May 27th 1972

A few months before going into Exile

He carried the book in a cream cardboard box

As he bounced between Europe

And the United States

In the Seventies Eighties

One day

While deplaning in Amsterdam

He realized

His Masterpiece was missing

And for several years

He carried its Loss

From city to city

In a battered travel bag

Knowing he could never duplicate

The feel or precision of the Pages

One crystalline Spring in Milan

He comes across the crushed box

In Alberto Giussani's attic

And decides to leave it there

After a few more years of drifting

Johns is back in Milan

Teaching golf in a tanning parlor

When good Luck strikes

One of his students

Is the Director of Jackson Libri

A booming house of informatica

Paolo Reina's intrigued

By his transvaluation of numbers

And publishes Sensazioni in 1993

With an Italian introduction

A transparent plastic insert

To overlay the grammar

The first hardback edition

Is numbered to 1000

It arrives in three print versions

Black

Blue

Ferrari Red

Senzazioni is first presented

In the small village

Of Castiglione di Sicilia that summer

Where Johns is working

As the professional

At Il Piccolo Golf Club

After the teenage daughter of a member

Sings a selection of Verdi arias

The future success of the book

Is celebrated with overflowing plates

Of pasta norma and local red wine

I've studied the 28 extant copies

Of the Jackson Libri first edition

That survived the Chaos of the Restoration

Like Monet's haystacks mutating

In the setting sun

I found many subtle differences

In the reading Experience

Moving from color to color

I've also watched the five-hour film version

Johns made with Paul Flum in 2018

And discovered with some surprise

That my Brain

Supplied a different soundtrack

To each new viewing

I heard the frogs

I heard the car crash

I heard my favorite saxophone solo

Mastering the positional grammar

Of Universal Field Language

Takes twenty minutes

With practice

You can read a page in a glance

Or follow selected columns and rows

Like characters in a novel

You can focus on specific squares

Think of them as individual synapses

Receiving competing streams of data

It's a silent language

That shouts out many Interpretations

Many subconscious Messages

For all its aesthetic appeal

And conceptual originality

I think the primary value of Sensazioni

Is the Shock it gives to inherited Concepts

In Western Philosophy and Psychology

That carry the heavy baggage

Of assumptions about Reality

Derived from modern languages

Based on Greek and Latin

Once Truth is freed

From the way you learned to learn

Objective Knowledge of the World

Becomes a real Possibility

University neuroscientists have confirmed

Two central themes of Sensazioni

The Eye

And Advanced Survival Consciousness

Are clearly the two dominant Drivers

Of Human Reality

Over the span of 4 billion years

They've defeated and suppressed

All their sensory and conscious Rivals

What would Man be today

If the Eye wasn't in Control?

If Advanced Survival wasn't the Goal?

Could Sensazioni be a modern alchemic text?

A marble stele left standing in the desert

Of Twentieth Century literature

Celebrating a battlefield Victory

That few will acknowledge

And Nobody will ever decipher?

On Texas Red

To honor the great Expressions
Of the European Artists
That inspired you to think
In pure Colors
And compressed Space
You lasso their Masterpieces
And bring them out to your Ranch
Close to midnight
Around a small mesquite fire
Close to midnight
With the rolling fumes
Framing the glowing hot irons
You burn their best paintings
With your Rocking T R brand
The screams are brief
And they get to their feet
Astonished by your audacity
Your stenciled Ego on Canvas
They snap back to their places

In the Western Pantheon

Tell their friends

It's just a tattoo

I picked up in Singapore

It's just a tattoo

I picked up in the Russian gulag

To remind me of my Lost Years

After some Time

After some Distance

The T R brand on their skin

Is covered by patina and lichen

They say

Sure

I knew Texas Red

Back in those crazy years

Before the Restoration

I was with him for a month in New York

When Banksy did the Street Exhibition

The media driven Treasure Hunt

When Banksy hired a codger to sell Originals

Outside the Met for sixty dollars

I drove T R to Home Depot

To buy his Rust-Oleum spray cans

I drove T R to Goodwill

To buy his slappy used canvases

I helped him cut his cardboard stencils

He was branding his favorite Masters

Until The Delusion Of Distance

Changed the Workings of the World

And pulled him deep into Abstraction

In The Reading Room

After the virus runs its course

Talezen rides the welcome rays

Of returning health

Straight to the Museum Library

He's met in the Reading Room

By Pembrey

Polyhistor

Short

Pencil thin

Cropped white hair

Sporting a burgundy velvet jacket

A brief moustache

He points to stacks of papers books

On the long teak table

Offers a small glass of sherry

Brings out the white cotton gloves

Talezen

Your timing is excellent

I'm preparing an exhibition

Of Johns' literary works

That will be accompanied

By a weekly series of lectures

The Western Way was instrumental

To the founding of Athenapolis

Important lines of the epic poem

Have been memorized

By every University student

My biographical talks

On his early experimental

And unpublished works

Will reveal new perspectives

On the epic Poem

That inspired the Restoration

It's well documented

That beyond a small circle

Of Family and Friends

Johns was unknown in his time

No major publisher

No national reading tours

No high volume podcasts

As the Prime Observer of his Life

He never considers writing a career

He never considers any career

Worthy of his time or attention

He lives in a 1960 Ford Econoline van

For four carefree years

Plays draw poker in Gardena casinos

Whenever he passes through California

He enjoys the transatlantic tango

For fifteen years

Relying on his wits

And splendid good Luck

To surf sofas and chance encounters

Into his Forties

He only writes

When he feels like it

Or when possessed by his Muse

There are enormous Voids in his Life

When he writes Nothing

Or just romantic ditties

Scribbled on napkins

Left to flutter towards a smile

A lift to a French Chateau

I've studied Sensazioni

Talezen says

Good

That book astounded him for decades

He never completely decoded it

He toyed with the grammar

Changed the title

Retrofitted major concepts

From his later Philosophy

But always returned

To the Jackson Libri version

In 1972

A few weeks after inventing

Universal Field Language

For Sensazioni

He writes a Yellow Diamond

A 19 page Beauty

In modified UFL

Pembrey takes a creased manila folder

From the stack

This is

The Assassination Of Buddha By His Daughter

Notice

The handwritten introduction

Written on a legal pad

He claims the traditional story

Of Buddha's accidental death by mushrooms

Is a religious Lie

Recounted over the centuries

For reasons deliberately lost

According to Johns

The real story

Is that Buddha was killed

By the Daughter

He abandoned at the royal palace

When he renounced the World

When he joined the wandering saddhus

Johns places the Mind

Body

Spirit

Of Buddha

Here on the left side of the page

The Daughter's

On the right

The seven levels of Consciousness

Are carried over from Sensazioni

And the mint green graph paper

Is from the same stock

Still influenced by the Eight Legs

Johns writes Chinese ideograms

For the main numbers

Arabic numbers in blue and red

For the subscripts

In Sensazioni Johns tells the story

Of all the Major Events

In the History of Consciousness

In The Assassination Of Buddha By His Daughter

He tells the story of a single Major Event

In the History of India

The Daughter symbolizes

The traditional Hindu religion

Of Reincarnations

Elaborate Rituals

Absolute Devotion

In 19 pages

Johns describes how the Hindu priests

Saw Buddha as a threat to their Power

Gave him the poisoned mushrooms

This explains why Buddhism

Was expelled from India

Shortly after Buddha's Death

For demolishing the Hindu Dogmas

Brokered by the powerful Brahmins

Here

On page 14

The main numbers

Change to Arabic

And here

After page 18

Page 19 is missing

I've concluded

By an analysis of the text

By comparison to the blank pages

In Sensazioni

That the gap is a clue

To suppressed passages of the Story

Our manuscript

Of The Assassination

Is the original

It was never photocopied or published

I assume it was highly prized

By Johns

Because it survived the Confusion

That accompanied the Restoration

Pembrey adds sotto voce

I find it intriguing

That after writing an abstract

History of Everything

Johns felt the need to focus

On a single Indian Event

What difference does it make

How Buddha died?

What possible relevance could it have

To Western Philosophy Theology?

The answer could come from Hong Kong

In the years 1967-68

When he studied Buddhism

With the Chan Master Y L Yen

His instant understanding of Nothingness

Of the Southern School meditation technique

Lay dormant for five years

To emerge from a causal chain

If Buddha hadn't been murdered

If Buddhism hadn't be expelled from India

If Bodhidarma hadn't brought Chan to China

If Hui Neng hadn't refined it in the South

If Y L Yen hadn't taught it in Hong Kong

Then Johns wouldn't have received

The Chan Transmission

At the age of 21

In The Western Way he views Buddha

As his second Worthy Opponent

This makes me think The Assassination

Is Johns' written confession

To the murder of Buddha

So he could break with his Chan Teacher

And Buddhist Nothingness

To create a new Philosophy

Of his own device

Walking Up Down the World

Would you like a refill?

As Pembrey leaves the room

Talezen touches turns the pages

Thinking that for two millennia

Western Culture's been dominated

By the Death of Jesus

And the possibility he was murdered

By jealous Jewish priests

Yet Christian Faith has never claimed

Or considered That Death an accident

Pembrey returns with a dark bottle

Wrapped in sackcloth

Fills the tiny glasses

Pulls out Yellow Roses

Here's another handwritten original

Written in a sketchy version of UFL

Dated October 16 1972

Hardbound at Kinko's

Yellow Roses is aesthetic arcane

Each cardinal number is a yellow rose

Commanding a space on the page

The main number in the square

Indicates the Intensity

Of the number's fragrance

Of the esoteric Emanation
The eight positions around the square
Indicate the Eight Unnamed Thoughts
As rose petals
Opening into Higher Consciousness
With their subscripts
Reporting their degree of expansion
The premise of Yellow Roses
Is clearly Pythagorean
All Mind
And all the Material World it imagines
Is derived from the nine cardinal numbers
The Eight primary Thoughts
Are left unnamed for the uninitiated
While their direct Influences
On Higher Consciousness
Are documented for the Few
Numbers are Roses
Fragrance leads to Knowledge
And the Flowering of the Mind
Has precise numerological roots
In the 149 pages of Yellow Roses

Johns passes from the translation

Of quantitative to qualitative

Into Hermetic symbolism

That matches the Eight Unnamed Thoughts

With the Eight Frequencies of the World

Next

We have a Blank

Pembrey slides a plastic folder

Across the table

Containing a page with two words

Maggie's Rage

As far as we know

This work no longer exists

All we have is a tape recording

Made by Johns' friend Joseph Ross

That mentions handwritten numbers

On a Grid

Eight columns representing

Eight friends at a Laurel Canyon party

That degenerates into shock

And violence

When one girl is unmasked as a Nark

The only reason I keep this title

In the Johns Archive

Is because it presages Dessy Cardoza

The Dark Lady in Love And Hate

And Beyond Exile

Allow me

Pembrey refills Talezen's glass

Continues

We don't know how many books

Johns wrote in UFL

That were lost or destroyed

In his wandering years

In 1973 Johns took a leave of absence

From the Graduate Theological Union

Traveled to Italy

England

France

Germany

Then a tour of India

Nepal

Thailand

Hong Kong

Bali

Singapore

Collecting Tibetan tankas

Chinese graveyard porcelain

He hitchhiked through Mexico

With girlfriend Silva Gianni

Eventually returned to Berkeley

In 1975

To write his dissertation

Andy Warhol: A Radical Theological Study

And receive the Ph. D degree

In Theology and The Arts from GTU

In the summer of 1976

He's immediately back in Europe

Shuttling between Italy and Germany

And the next work we have

Is the bizarre Weaselskin

Another handwritten manuscript

Written in modified UFL

On white graph paper

Dated 1976 in Cologne

This book is an outlier for several reasons

The introduction is a poetic hymn

To Eternal Recurrence

To Affirmation of The Moment

As Ducks on the Water

Arousing the Arrows of Passion

The weasel's skin

Is the exposed flesh

Of the Eternal Sun

That rises with every Erection

And defies Time in every Climax

Power

Rage

Jealousy

Ecstasy

Are the Four Elements

Of the basic grammar

The 123 pages

Written in black and red markers

Are a sequence of expressionistic sketches

Dominated by the persistence

Of the Number 2

And the Actions of the Arrows

It's a private document

Of his affair with the German librarian

Beatrix Alexander

It's symbolic erotica

And Weaselskin attracts aficionados

Of Frank Harris

Henry Miller

But it lacks the intellectual depth

Or literary power

Of his earlier UFL works

It's a diary

A mannerist Gesture

A blue polaroid

Celebrating incandescent sex

That I plan to exhibit this once

Then return to the vault

Around 1980

Johns returned to California

To the poker life

He was living in the early 70s

He takes a small room

At the trucker hooker Key Hotel

In Emeryville

It has purple orchid wallpaper

A private view of the ventilation shaft

He plays the quarter ante no limit

Five-card draw table

In the back of the Key Club bar

The Joker goes with aces

Straights

And flushes

He grinds the drug dealers

Long haul truckers

Cocky Black pimps

Until 6 AM

Then it's Rainer Ale from Rollie's Liquor

A double cheese

From the Doggie Diner

Before crashing on the antique bed

In Room 218

To the sound of gunshots down the hall

Afternoons evenings

He writes two mammoth novels

A fistful of short stories

That he scientifically edits down

To crushed paper balls

Dropped down the stinking shaft

Or casually slipped into the gutter

On San Pablo Avenue

On his way to breakfast

Scrambled eggs grits toast

At the Happy Sunshine Cafe

He's in Santa Cruz

Flipping classic cars

When he meets Fred Park

Hitting sand shots on the beach

They decide to start a golf school

In LA

Fred immediately gets busted

For a bad heroin Habit

And a sequence of bad Decisions

So in 1985

Johns launches the school solo

Plays Yamaha clubs in local pro events

Writes philosophical speculations

In suburban Yorba Linda

We have two clean copies

Of Pentheus and Dionysus

Written on electric typewriter

91 paragraphs of observations

Opinions

Literary references

Based on the division of Man

Into three Types

Skaters

Suckers

Snitches

It has occasional brilliance

Glimpses of the laconic style

In his later writings

But it's clearly a working draft

A preliminary dialog with favorite authors

That was never edited or polished

During this LA golf school parenthesis

Johns writes a larger philosophical piece

With sharper objectives

Titled Singularities

671 Aphorisms

Miscellaneous maxims

Cultural observations

That expand the scope of his Investigations

That contain some conceptual seeds

Later refined and inserted

Into the radical soil of his Epic Poems

By late 1988

Johns is back in Italy

Promised a golf pro job

At a club in Alessandria

That never materializes

He recovers in the small Tuscan village

Of Equi Termi

After three weeks of sulfur baths

He meets the beautiful charming

Scintillating Cristina Tacconi

On a blind date by the river Po

Falls madly In Love

And proposes seven days later

While she's studying

For her journalism exams

He writes The Philosophy Of Golf

93 pages of typescript

This original study

On the mental side of the game

Is the primary theoretical source

For his Golf Strategy essay

Published in 2011

In 1989

He marries Cristina in Portland

First at the Multnomah County courthouse

Then at Oraibi

On the Hopi Indian Reservation

In Northern Arizona

Dousing their heads

With kernels of sacred yellow corn

The steady clammy Oregon rain

And diminishing prospects

Stimulate their return to Milan

In 1992 Johns is hired

As a consultant

To assist the opening

Of the Marco Simone Golf Club

Outside of Rome

After nine months of dysfunction

Written in streaming bile by Kafka

He's stabbed in the back

And abruptly dismissed

By Laura Biagiotti

Spring of 1993

Finds him in Sicily

Teaching golf

On the shoulders of Mt Etna

His marvelous next work

The Road To Eleusis

Is completed in a sprawling villa

Surrounded by exotic citrus trees

On a bluff above Fiumefreddo

The Road

Is a new variant of UFL

And a fine example of its great promise

373 pages

Written in colored markers

The premise is Two Lovers

On a long motor tour of Europe

That ends at the Eleusinian Mysteries

Around 449 BC

Each rectangle is subdivided

Into 15 squares

Housing the primary Greek gods

When a road sign appears

In a god's square

Roger

Fiammetta

Is possessed by that god

We have dual possessions

Multiple possessions

Competing possessions

We have a raging river of possessions

On this long European road trip

Whenever you see a road sign

A Divine Invasion occurs

Here

On Page 36

Between Geneva and Paris

The road sign of Men Working

Appears in Roger's Dionysus square

He's instantly overwhelmed

Loses control of the steering wheel

Careens into a fetid ditch

When Talezen sees the red triangle

At the tip of Pembrey's finger

He's instantly overcome by nausea

Roaring vertigo

He tries to stand up

But twists awkwardly to the floor

The Reading Room is swirling

In a brown tornado of books

Shelves

Library ladders

Then

Just as suddenly

It passes

Pembrey's wiping his brow

With a white cotton handkerchief

Talezen's sitting up

Fixing his gaze on a row

Of Plutarch's Lives

To stop the spinning world

I'm OK

He says

I know what it is

I went to Byd

And met Iggy

Yes

The Infant God

Says Pembrey

He jumped into my Weaselskin

And made my life a Mess

Pembrey smiles at the humor

Talezen

We can continue another day

I'm fine now

He's leaning on the table

Wondering

But knowing deep inside the wonder

Why Dionysus was the trigger

Of this attack

Pembrey

Let's carry on

As you like

Permbrey slides The Road To Eleusis

To the end of the table

Fetches tall glasses of glacier water

Continues

In the spring of 1994

Johns returns to Portland

With his pregnant wife Cristina

Their son Clarence is born June 28th

Johns starts a new golf school

At Persimmon Golf Club

Has a golf talk show on radio

With Pat Fitzsimons

It's during this happy period

Bringing up the baby

Relaxing as a revenant

Of his extended European Exile

That Johns decides to be

What he always was

A poet

He was the campus poet at UC Riverside

He was the resident poet at GTU

He's spent fifteen years as a golf pro

Twenty years writing experimental books

Now's the time to affirm

To return to his True Being

It's torture

It consumes all his time and attention

It takes him kalpas to find the right Voice

It takes him kalpas to find the right Form

Nothing works

And his marriage is fracturing

Without reason or recourse

He writes through the Distress

The lawyers and letters

The arguments and scenes

Nothing works

He continues to seek the right Expression

Of his most natural Nature

As the divorce grinds on

None of it is any good

None of it is going anywhere

He has hundreds of pages of trash

But his Will is strong

Stronger than ever

Poet

Is the catalyst and synthesis

Of his most inner Identity

His chosen Destiny

He despises all confessional poetry

Stemming from Whitman

He hates the poetry magazines

For their fey gratuitous pandering

He wants to honor Homer

The ancient Welsh bards

He's thinking of a modern Epic

Without regular rhyme or meter

Without standard punctuation

That tells of heroic Personalities

Historic deeds

Impossible love affairs

But what Personalities?

What deeds?

He's been living in Europe

Dreaming in German and Italian

Now he's back in the States

Trying to recover his English style

What Personalities?

What deeds?

Then finally it clicks

The Time is the late Sixties

The Place is Haight Ashbury

The Heart of the Counterculture

The Birth of the Summer of Love

He'll tell the story

Of two friends who didn't survive

The Revolution That Failed

He'll tell of the Diggers

Of their radical free store

Free food

Free crashpad

Social action programs

He's got the Subject

But the Words still don't flow

Every draft comes out lame

Or gutted by angry editing

So when his golf school

Is dropped by Persimmon

He enters the world of luxury car sales

And puts the manuscript away

In 2000 he founds Conscious Publishing

To bring out Science And Myth

For his friend Gianfranco Spavieri

The Italian physicist he met

Playing ping pong at UCR

And The Golden Vortex

By Nick Nelson

The tour guide

Independent researcher

Of electromagnetism

Met at the Oregon Vortex in Gold Hill

On a summer vacation with Clarence

In 2003 he co-founds the Portland Alien Museum

With his friend Steve Hanns

Nick Nelson installs a vortex anomaly

On the front porch

PAM has running videos of crop circles

An extensive UFO research library

A 3-D alien rollercoaster in the back room

Displays of the Nine Alien Types

A popular series of Guest Lectures

At 9

Clarence is the Museum Director

Moving visitors through the rooms

With courteous alacrity clever patter

PAM has international Success

Interviews with Paris Match the BBC

A big spot on Google Maps

Rave recommendations

In 55 national Sunday supplements

But after the short Portland tourist season

The museum's leaking oil

They've attracted the attention

Of certain Black Agencies

And a toxic cloud of lunatics

With abduction tales fake artifacts

So they shut it down

After PAM

Johns' search for a modern poetic Form

Continues to lurch in the alleys

Of his Frustration

Until he sees Billy Collins

His witty partner in Acid Adventures

In the late Sixties early Seventies

On the cover of Poetry Magazine

Smiling as America's Poet Laureate

When they hung out together

Lawrence was the Poet

Billy the UCR Teaching Assistant

Hunter College Professor

After thirty years of Playing the Game

To get his unique Voice recognized

Through connections key publications

Billy becomes the Face

Of American Poetry

For his lyric Hospitality

Zen Humor

Astronomical sales

This was the Jolt he needed

A quick glance tells him

That Billy's kind invitations

To enter the first lines of his poems

His genuine humanity in the middle lines

And his focus on the transcendence

Of everyday events at the wire

Gives him an inexhaustible source

Of popularity with American readers

In his radical heart

Johns has a different Goal

He'll modify the Past

To imprint his Vision on the Future

Like the cartoon show for prisoners

In Sullivan's Travels

Billy's poems serve the High Purpose

Of providing temporary Comic Relief

From the Reality of chain gang America

He'll write Tragedies to force Catharsis

Break the steel links to this Dominant Reality

Expose the government's sadistic Need

To mow down the Flower Revolution

He assembles a strong cast of characters

He investigates the English Diggers

Ken Kesey the Merry Pranksters

The Black Panthers

The San Francisco Bands

The plans of the FBI

To discredit dismember the Hippies

Once his Intent is clear

The poetic Form emerges

From a labyrinth of speculations

From dead time on the Cadillac lot

He'll tell the story

Of the Rise and Fall of Haight Ashbury

He'll tell of Rare Beauties

Exciting Freedoms

Fatal Infiltrations

He'll reintroduce the Epic Form

To Modern Poetry

He'll rewrite American History

To defuse the fascist dystopian Future

Planned by the Commerce Class

The Diggers saved hundreds of runaways

From prostitution and worse

But they were easily compromised

The FBI covert operation

Called the Death Of Hippie

Was produced by Dessy Cardoza

Promoted by national TV coverage

Of crazed brunette runaways

Jumping from high Victorian windows

Conscious Publishing

Brings out Love And Hate

In 2005

The cryptic lines

The intensely visual metaphors

Give it the feel of a screenplay

Starring Young Love

And Reckless Rebellion

For the cover

Billy writes

Heads of acid roll again

This time in verse

The historian Michael William Doyle

Writes that Love And Hate

Is the best fiction written

On The Sixties

Naming Lawrence Johns

Poet Laureate of the Counterculture

Its first public presentation

Is at the Ground Zero Lounge

In downtown Portland

Where Johns is doing standup

With Clyde Lewis

After Paul Flum finishes a calzone

He receives the first signed copy

Johns reads Dig The Diggers

On a Portland radio show

Hosted by Josie

One of the original Diggers

From the San Francisco Mime Troupe

She praises the trickster Style

But claims it warps

What really went down

Emmett Grogan was a heavy Junkie

Fucked up Everything all the time

Peter Berg only cared about Peter

And his public image as a community organizer

This is when Johns says on the air

You may have lived it

But all memory fades

Future generations will remember the Haight

Exactly how I describe it here

The function of Poetry is to improve Reality

Not to praise or reproduce it

He makes a brief tour

Of the Portland bookstores

Libraries

Reading selections to gray hippies

In ponytails and tie-dyed t shirts

Platinum ladies staring at the ceiling

Luxuriating in mistaken aural pleasures

Peter Coyote likes it

Peter Berg won't discuss the Diggers

Or anything to do with the Sixties

Because he's promoting urban ecology

Emmett Grogan's long dead

From an overdose on the F train

On Staten Island

Johns soon tires of book promotion

He has the right Form

He has the right Energy

It's time to write a new Epic Poem

But what new Personalities?

What new deeds?

He lifts Frank Glendover

From the Love And Hate ensemble

Creates a mythology of the Seventies

In the grip of international terrorism

He creates an occult Personality

For Carlos The Jackal

He puts Frank under watch

By Dessy and the CIA

Makes him run blind

Through a series of Mistakes

Misfortunes

Near-Death Experiences

Makes him fight a Duel of Archetypes

On the torrid Mediterranean stage

Carlos is Thelema Magick

Frank is Nietzschean Truth

They meet

And they meet again

Their personal contest concludes in Libya

At the Mountains of the Moon

With the New Babylon Working

When Frank drops his gun in the sand

Conscious Publishing

Brings out Beyond Exile in 2008

It gives romantic political gloss

To the tumultuous terrorist Seventies

It gives illuminating cameos

To Jack Parsons and L Ron Hubbard

Chiaroscuro

To the grimoires of Alistair Crowley

And paints a radical portrait of Carlos

The man who carried three names of Lenin

Into running battle with the West

At the height of the Cold War

Soon

Paul Flum creates a video game version

Of Beyond Exile

That becomes the springboard

For 39 episodes of the TV Series

I'm Carlos Now

After redefining the Sixties and Seventies

To match his Theories

Johns' discovery of Voletic Energy

Puts pause to his Poetry

While he concentrates

On his Explorations in The Deep

Next

We have the extravagant essay

That transformed the Homoborgs

Designer Linda Hurst

Adorns Golf Strategy

With Medieval iconography

Castles

Armor

Swords

Tournament jousts

Leap from the facing pages

To illustrate Johns' contention

That the True Golfer

Must be both a Lover and a Knight

The final section is a satirical account

Of the Grand Strategist

Caddying for his best student

In a national championship

Forced to witness

Every element of his Strategy

Ignored

Undermined

Refuted in the final nine holes
The essay has obvious merit
For relieving mental pressure in competition
For making each shot selection automatic
Based on the most recent results
But it jumps and swerves
In many directions at once
It doesn't have an Image of a golfer
A golf course
Or a golf club
To double down on the crime
Johns puts his ancestral coat of arms
The Three Ravens
On the front cover
The prose wanders more than Carlyle
More than Montaigne
The sound advice for practice
And competitive tournament play
Is quickly lost in a wooly mix
Of obscure historical anecdotes
And absurd shotmaking situations
Conscious Publishing

Brings it out hardback

In 2011

Although I haven't verified the sale

Of a single copy

Golf Strategy may turn out to be the book

With the greatest influence on the Future

Because billions of Homoborgs

Currently use it for their Life Strategy

Talezen

How are you feeling?

I'm fine

Pembrey

How did you get the material

For this exhibition?

I've been writing papers on Johns

Since 9th grade

Never found this wealth of detail

Talezen

By longstanding Museum Library protocol

Certain critical Information

Can only be transmitted verbally

However

Your interest in Johns

Hasn't gone unnoticed

One member of the Council

Contends you are the Continuation

Of his Will-Based Soul

I've yet to decide this point

But I wouldn't put it past Johns

To figure out a way to live the Flesh

Of the Perfect Society he created by Mind

I also think some of these personal facts

May be familiar to you

I've always felt

A certain fluidity

A certain Universality of Self

Replies Talezen

I'm everything that's young

I'm everything that's old

I'm every predator

I'm every prey

But I'm certainly not Johns

I could never recreate his mix

Of remarkable good Luck

And psychic connection to Greek Tragedy

Most of my poems are a single line

My Mind works best

When optimizing a single Action

Myth is the mirror

Of our future Metaphor

Says Pembrey at the front door

Steal from Johns what you need

Good afternoon Pembrey

Break a leg Talezen

The City awaits your Performance

Three Announcements

Metis claps his hands

To acknowledge the warm applause

As he strides to the granite podium

In the Rhodri Theater

My Sagaxi

Walk with me back in time

We're in the Panhandle

Of San Franscisco

We're approaching the pots

Of bubbling beef stew

We can smell the onions

Carrots potatoes

A young man is juggling crystal balls

A young woman is singing French airs

Before joining the line

We must enter

A tall Frame of Reference

Made of rough two by fours

Painted bright yellow

The Diggers have symbolized

The Transition to Free City

With a simple wooden Rectangle

We step through

And join the happy faces

Waiting with chipped sundry bowls

For free dinner in the Haight

Now

Fast forward

To the Restoration

And the founding of Athenapolis

We took the evolutionary Leap

We became Homosagax

Developing new mental Powers

New Fields of Action

For our High Intelligence

Parents in the audience

Who have Eighth Graders at home

Understand this Unfolding

We stand at the Peak of Human History

We have Power with Wisdom

But any slip can result in Avalanche

We saw this in Dalarick's Revolt

We see this today

In the crass machinations

Of the Count of Verona

This is why

We must protect the City's Freedom

With all our combined Powers

This is why I favor

The systems analysis of Wissner-Gross

Formulated in the early days of A I

Over Talezen's Mechanics of Third Will

Like a game of go with many branches

Like slime mold looking for food

Like the spread of Filaments

In the vast Cosmic Web

The Force of Intelligence

Maximizes the Freedom of Future Action

By keeping every Option open

It evades all stagnation

All loops

All dead ends

Talezen's assumptions

That More Intelligence is the Goal of Intelligence
That Problem-Solving is its Main Function
Are partially true and totally skeletal
The Force of Intelligence sets many Goals
In multiple Fields
When every Option is kept open
Fewer Big Problems arise
And Survival is more assured
In Three Will Theory
Being is Action
So it makes Sense
For the Force of Intelligence
To prefer the generation of New Being
Over solutions to ever tougher Problems
Clearly
The true odds of a Free Future
Are Zero
Without the Council
Selecting the optimal Action
From the large number of Options
Because Wissner-Gross' attempt to establish
A single underlying formula

To describe the Mechanics of Intelligence
Was initially intended for A I programming
It can be easily adapted to provide
A reliable Framework for the Council
In the selection of the Action
That creates the most future Possibilities
My Sagaxi
A Major Threat
To our Free Future is upon us
We must be alert
Like naked Nature
Courageous
Like our Ancestors
When they overthrew the Commerce Class
Confident
Like the first Excitations
Of Western Enlightenment
My Sagaxi
I was hiking to the Bear Mountain shack
For a week of Voletic Meditation
When the Challenge came
I was tired sweaty wet

When this Darkness

Walked right through me

Its Identity was obscured

Its Identity was well known

The fangs of its Dark Shadow

Still rip flesh in my Dreams

It operates under many Names

Many Masks

In the History of Western Culture

It's been called the Prince of Darkness

Satan

Older Brother

Traditionally and falsely considered

A disembodied Spirt by Abrahamic religions

We now have a better

A more accurate description

Our perennial Adversary

Is the Physical Manifestation

Of Second Will

Another Cosmos in the Multiverse

Jealous

Enraged

By our Sensational Love

By the Achievements of our Advanced Minds

Another Cosmos

Driven by Hate and Envy

To drop Our World

Into its lowest energy state

No Fire

No Ice

Just instant Return

To the No Time before Time

To the Non Being before Being

My Sagaxi

I've been challenged to Single Combat

By this Enemy

And I've accepted

Had I declined

Our Freedom of Action

In every near and distant Future

Would be severely compromised

Could it be a trap?

A bluff?

Could it be my subconscious Projection

In a difficult personal Moment?

Perhaps

But we must take this Risk

We must defend Athenapolis

Throughout all Spacetime

We're still building out God's Brain

We're still bringing the Universe

To Self-Consciousness

Yes

Everything's running fine

Yes

Earth's a Garden again

But now

To succeed in this defining Moment

We need to raise our Consciousness

Beyond the Advanced Mind

Into Unity with the First Will Imperative

My Sagaxi

This Challenge may be the Opportunity

To free our Nightmares

From the parasitic Negativity

The Nostalgia for Non Being

That's been interfering with our Progress

Since we left the ancestral forest

And began to walk upright

It's not a Spirit

Or Ghost

Distilled from Sapiens Ignorance

Fear

Faith

It's a purely corporal Opponent

We're stronger

Smarter

More resourceful

Than any other living Being

We can handle This

We've done it a hundred times before

My Sagaxi

I'll defeat this Darkness

And the World will continue to hum along

In its optimal energy state

All will be Well

As Metis pauses

For a sip of water

White silence shakes the Theater

Followed by a cacophony of questions

As the Derwids replay his statements

Looking for nuances

Ironies

Codewords indicating

His Announcement

Was performance or rhetorical Art

But quickly conclude

If a Challenge was issued

Then Metis is our Champion

A baby cries

Another baby cries

Somebody coughs

All eyes are fixed on his face

As Metis continues

My Sagaxi

I have two more announcements

The Homoborgs

Have changed their name

They will now be known as Vardons

In honor of the ancient English golfer

Lastly

The first Be-In

Will be held on the third Saturday of July

On the Athenaid grounds

All Four Classes have been invited

And impromptu displays

Of Communication and Understanding

Are officially encouraged

After returning from the Fight

Outside the World

I'll give a Mountain Talk

At the Festival

An hour before Sunset

My Sagaxi

Stay True to the Earth

Maximize your Possibilities

And keep an Eye

On the Eighth Graders

They're planning Something

That could alter the Course of Time

Now Metis pauses

Now Metis hits his chest with both fists

192

Now Metis raises his arms in Victory

And walks briskly Out

Sourwood Honey

Pembrey takes the small stage

In the Millbrook backyard

Dressed in a cream linen suit

It's late June

It's hot

The students are in shorts

Psychedelic t shirts

Holding hands

In the folding camp chairs

You know these Poems quite well

Begins Pembrey

So today I'll relate some new details

You didn't learn in class

Firstly

We owe the creation of The Western Way

To an Eastern virus

In late 2019

An American designed and funded

Bioweapon project

In Wuhan China

Produced a new military virus

That escaped the lab

And quickly infected the world's population

In its early stage COVID 19 killed

Ten thousand a week in New York City

It would rage on to take 18 million lives

Handicap another 40 million worldwide

Forced into extreme isolation

By the state of his immune system

Lawrence Johns decides to write down

His most explosive Ideas

As a Document

Addressed expressly to you

His future Audience

The students of his time were brainwashed

By political economic ideologies

Designed to groom them

Into highly productive components

Of the Commerce Class Machine

To systematically suffocate

Their natural Empathy and Idealism

In counterattack

Johns writes The Western Way

To distinguish Western Enlightenment

From the Eastern Ways of India and China

Coopted by American corporations

To marginalize minimalize the Individual

To train absolute dependence on the Group

He differentiates his Philosophy

From the European Age of Enlightenment

In the 17th and 18th Centuries

Initiated by Locke

Bacon

D'Alembert

Voltaire

Diderot

That established a secular Cult of Reason

And transferred Power to the Commerce Class

In the Industrial Revolutions

Of the 19th and 20th Centuries

From his Portland apartment

Overlooking a small creek

Flanked by flailing willows

Crackling with squirrels

Bickering crows

Cruising mallard ducks

Johns sees the United States

Crippled by its corrupt health system

Stumbling in pandemic panic

He sees a reprise of the Black Death

When 14th Century European Intelligence

Left the contagious Cities

And made for the Mountains

He sees how Reason was kidnapped

Raped

Mutilated

Mocked

In the 21st Century

By the massive propaganda Power

And technological Reach

Of the ruling Commerce Class

How Reason proved too feeble

Too slow

Too dialectically flexible

To defend the Future of American Society

Against the escalating wealth of billionaires

And their greedy swarm of political sycophants

When Johns was writing The Western Way

Young Americans were expected to adopt

The New Medieval mentalities

Of passivity and resignation

When using their computers

Smart phones

Social media

A I Agents

Initially introduced as Fun and Games

American High Technology quickly became

The Electronic Harness of the Corporate State

Critical Thinking

Reading faces

Reading body language

Understanding the Other

Became antiquated irrelevant

In a mad and hostile World

The Self-Determination of the Self

So fresh and vital for Kant

So essential for Nietzsche

Was supplanted by submissive Groups

Of consumers

Voters

Workers

Identified by algorithms

Categorized by algorithms

Bought and sold by algorithms

That reduced their Individuality to habits

And polished the jackboot on their throats

Johns' answer to this Easting of the West

Was to redefine Western Enlightenment

In terms of Three Will Theory

Infant God Theory

The Will-Based Soul

The Restoration of the Wisdom Class

In Seventh Grade you learned

How Johns takes Will from Schopenhauer

Runs it by Nietzsche

And splits it into three competing Forces

A First Will drive for more Life

A Second Will drive for more Death

And a Third Will drive for more Intelligence

That can align with both First and Second Will

All Nature

All human Psychology

Exhibits the dynamic interactions

Between these Three Forces

In Johns' extension of Nietzsche

The Will-Based Enlightenment

Described in The Western Way

Is more fundamental more robust

Than any system based on Reason

Students of Summer

Athenapolis

The City of your Birth and Growth

The steady source of your Energy

Is not a Rational Project

It's Instinctual

Earthly

Extemporaneous by design

How did the Commerce Class fall?

Was there a Gold Con?

Was there a Weapon?

We just don't know

The City's leadership has been prophetic

The City's administration has been casual

The City expands

Like a tree branching to receive the Sun

Like a river sliding to the Sea

And like the shimmering cloak of Nature

It prefers to keep its secrets safe

Students of History

Conscious Publishing brings out

The Western Way in 2023

Will And Resistance in 2024

The Force Of Intelligence in 2025

In the latter two Epic Poems

Johns predicts many of the major Attacks

On the Serenity of Athenapolis

We've faced and defeated

In the last few turbulent years

Next

I'd like to examine a small detail

That's generally gone unnoticed

In The Western Way

Johns addresses you as Sagaxi

In his time

Nietzsche's Ubermensch

Had accreted far too much misconception

Had degenerated into comics cliche

So he pirated Homosagax from Cicero

To distinguish your Being

From the Being of Homosapiens

In the Poem he never explains

Why he changed the correct Latin plural

Sagaces to Sagaxi

I think

That by modifying the Latin

Into a new word that looks and sounds better

Johns imprinted his poetic Intent

Into your living Identities

In a philological sense

When you think of yourselves

As Sagaxi

When you call yourselves Sagaxi

You become his sons and daughters

You carry forward his love of Invention

Students of the Arts and Sciences

Some University scholars have questioned

The final third of The Western Way

After philosophical Discussion

And some autobiographical Events

Johns jumps into V Dome Explorations

And his meeting with the Infant God

These aren't literary fantasies

We have his personal notes

His flight logs

In the Museum Library archive

They match the text perfectly

I think his motivation

For dramatically changing the narrative

Was to convey something to you

His future Audience

Yes

Creating New Art and New Science is exciting

But strong Inspiration needs strong Experience

In the final sections of The Western Way

I think Johns is saying

Reach out for dangerous Adventures

Record everything you See and Do

Discover a new version of your Self

Discover a better version of the World

And test them in personal Experience

Lawrence Johns was a scientific mystic

The Infant God was an Idea

Before he met him on Byd

And

The Infant God became an Idea

After he met him on Byd

This Paradox

This Plasticity of Time

This High Identity

Of Cause and Effect

Is key to the Understanding

Of Johns' literary Will

Remember

In The Western Way

Johns is talking to you as Sagaxi

As the Next Men

You'll soon be thinking things

That Man has never thought before

Doing things

That Man has never done before

In your psychedelic studies with Kendra

Here at Millbrook

You have the unique Opportunity

To fuse LSD and The Deep

To find a new Level of Consciousness

A revolutionary new literary Style

Remember

Every keen look into the Abyss

Can lead to Greatness

And sometimes

Just changing a suffix

Can change the Destiny of Man

After a tall glass of spring water

And twenty minutes

Of sharp orthogonal questions

Pembrey joins Kendra

Under a pearl white umbrella

On the blazing patio for tea

She pours double bergamot

Into small Sicilian cups

Silently applauding his talk

These kids are bonding well

She says

Handing Pembrey fresh butter

For the warm oosmos muffins

Pembrey leans smoothly down

Reaches into his satchel

Presents Kendra with a small jar

Of Appalachian sourwood honey

How thoughtful

How rare

She smells the caramel and gingerbread

Drips a spoonful on her muffin

Takes a dainty bite

Pembrey says

Talezen and Metis have opposing views

On the Force of Intelligence

Does it lead to more Problems

Or does it lead to more Possibilities?

The more I consider their positions

The more I alternate sides

Kendra

What do you think?

Third Will is never Free

It's always Bound

Always assisting accelerating

First or Second Will

So when the Force of Intelligence

Leads to Disease

Decay

Death

It's aligned with Second Will

And when it leads to Growth

New Horizons

New Life

It's aligned with First Will

Our most common

Our most existential case

Is when Third Will assists

First Will and Second Will simultaneously

With conflicting Energies that oscillate

In the wake of unpredictable Events

So I think the two perspectives

Describe dynamics of the same Reality
The Force of Intelligence
Creates a Life of Problems
And
A Life of Possibilities
In a Voletic Wave
Racing through cyclic Time
At or above the Speed of Light
Three Will Theory says
First Will always Wins Out
The fact that Everything We Know
And Everything We Can Know
Is still In Being
Confirms this superiority
But in the span of a single day
Third Will's acceleration
Of the degenerations destructions
Caused by Second Will
Can create such Despair
That Life appears to be a downward spiral
In the grip of the Death Wish
Elegant

Pembrey says

If Nature truly loves Equilibrium

Then the Force of Intelligence

May not be a separate Force at all

It could simply be the tendency

Of First and Second Wills

To exhaust themselves into Balance

Into Moderation

After a period of heated Excess

From this perspective the Gold Con

And the Weapon

Could simply be Inventions

Concealing the decisive Action

When Third Will rejoins First Will

In the High Moment of the Restoration

Kendra

These muffins are magnificent

And made irresponsibly transcendent

By the sourwood honey

She replies

As they sip their tea

And watch the students

Whizzing by on their bikes

The Be-In

Talezen's walking through the Rose Garden

On his way to the Be-In

When a jagged line cracks his vision

He feels a massive migraine coming on

The pain swells his forehead

Until it bursts an eagle

Flapping

Straight up

Out of Sight

He stumbles to a bench

Closes his eyes

Tries to calm the forked lightning

After ten minutes the crazy lines are gone

He slowly sits up

Appraising his situation

Iggy's gone!

No sign

No warning

Just gone!

How do I feel?

Not much different

Actually

I didn't ever feel much different

I knew he was there

Watching

Listening

Smelling

Tasting

Touching everything

We never really conversed

Or shared any thoughts

But every moment was intense

The highs and lows

Were titanic

Talezen pauses

Examines his forehead

With the restored fingers

Of his left hand

Everything's OK

No blood

No damage

Why now?

Why did Iggy leave me

Just before the Be-In?

Was he afraid of Something?

Or just done with Me

With the Character of Human Life?

Talezen continues down the gravel path

Letting the subtle tea scents

Provoke a sequence of positive Thoughts

Approaching the entrance

To the Athenaid grounds

He sees newsboys

Handing out special editions

With the schedule of Be-In Events

He sees thousands of light bulbs

Strung from hundreds of olive trees

Waiting for seductive dusk

And the Saturday evening festivities

He's surprised

To see so many Vardons

In Ralph Lauren Polos

Talking loud

Mingling large

Playing three miniature golf courses

With castles

Moats

Secret passageways leading

To elevated hidden cups

He sees Players in the logo t shirts

Of First Citizens Bank

Sanchez Realty

And other financial institutions

Carrying slim aluminum briefcases

Telling ribald jokes

Writing down the names of contacts

As he strolls past bamboo booths

Overflowing with animal ceramics

Talezen hears a bop jazz trio

A solo recorder

A swerving cloud of multicolor songbirds

He sees Players taking large bets

On Nobles playing lawn croquet

He sees Tullio with a gigantic Wicker Man

Standing on a steel stage with fresh tinder

And a large pile of white rocks

He's dressed in 17th century finery

A powder blue velvet justacorps

Over a flaming red silk waistcoat

Black silk breeches

A powdered white wig

He's addressing a cluster of Derwids

With missing front teeth

My Brothers!

My Worms!

Soon we'll cleanse this place of Filth!

Soon we'll bring this City to Sanity!

Soon your Support will shine in Posterity!

You see before you

The famous Wicker Man

The glorious Mock Ritual

Of the Celts

Your very grisly

Your very nasty Ancestors

Yes! My pitiful Worms!

Soon

One of you will enter his left leg
Through that little door
Be chained to the center post
And when I give the signal
Schopenhauer will light the Fire
Your personal Sacrifice
Will expose this Heresy of Nature
Called Athenapolis
And Man can return to Business as Usual
I can't accept a Noble
I can't accept a Player
I certainly can't accept a Vardon
No
Only a Derwid will do
One innocent Derwid
Will atone for the Many
Who've instituted the false flag
Of Individualism
And destroyed all True Ambition
One innocent Derwid
Will save the City from Sloth
Will save the City from the Folly

It calls the Western Way

From the obscene Pretense

It calls the Philosophy of Will

My lost and salacious Worms!

I lift you to the grass!

From the ashes of the Wicker Man

The only Society that works

The Nation State driven by Greed and Revenge

Will be reborn!

Taxes and police will be raised

To protect the rights of private property

The innocent Derwid

Who volunteers to mix his ashes

With the Wicker Man

Will remove the Wisdom Class

From their Counterfeit Power

And the Universe will rejoice!

O lovely day!

But what's this?

What Apparition approaches me?

A giant turtle bearing a golden crown

Emerges from behind the Wicker Man

Tullio makes a comic face of Recognition

Steps back

Grabs the crown

Puts it on his head

O Lovely Day!

The Count of Verona no more!

Now I am the Emperor of Earth!

Now I shake the Multiverse!

The crowd is a wide river of Vardons

Carrying islands of Nobles and Players

Enthusiastically to the stage

For my first Edict

I announce the royal distribution

Of our private property

All Derwids

Nobles

Players

And this luminescent sea of Vardons

Who swear a military Oath to Me

Will receive a white rock

From this hefty pile

You can exchange it

For tokens from First Citizens Bank

And buy any real estate you like

On planet Earth

Yes My precious Worms!

This is Democracy!

This is how we protect your Rights!

My second Edict

Appoints the Vardons

As the City's police force

Carlos!

Are you out there?

Carlos!

Come on up!

A husky middle-aged Vardon

Dressed in black linen

Touching his thick moustache

Separates calmly from his friends

Saunters towards the stage

With a sarcastic smile

Where's Frank?

He must be here somewhere

Carlos!

For your Magick behind the scenes

For your pivotal role in our Victory

Over the armies of Nihilism

I hereby name you Head of Palace Security

The assembled mass of Vardons

Raise a rolling cheer of approval

That's immediately silenced

By the sight of a second giant turtle

Emerging from behind the Wicker Man

Bearing a slender silver tiara

O Lovely Day!

My Brothers!

My Fat My Delicious Worms!

For my third Edict

I'm infinitely proud and humbled

To declare

That The Lady has consented

To be my Empress

With slow regal grace

Livia

Dressed in a simple turquoise wedding dress

Strides out from behind the Wicker Man

And stands beaming tall at Tullio's side
As he reaches up to place the crown
On her long blonde curls
Livia slowly waves her right hand
To her screaming hopping girlfriends
In this moment of High Exhilaration
Everybody is enchanted
Emotionally overwhelmed
Tuned to the pitch of High C
Schopenhauer!
Come up here!
The chimp emerges from beneath the stage
Wiping dust from his white satin tunic
Glaring at the first row of Vardons
Before jumping onstage for orders
Schopenhauer!
Prepare the bonfire!
As Schopenhauer props the tinder
Against the massive legs of the Wicker Man
Emperor Tullio and Empress Livia
Accept the whistling congratulations
The bouquets of morning wildflowers

Flung onstage by their followers

O Lovely Day!

OK!

Here we go!

Those ready to swear the Oath to me

Get in line over there

Good!

That's right!

Those ready to die in the Wicker Man

Get in line here

Beautiful!

Now

To be chosen as the Conscious Sacrifice

You must first answer this Riddle

What we catch

We throw away

What we don't catch

We carry with us

An embarrassing silence descends

Like a cold cloudburst on the crowd

After two long minutes

A sharp looking young Derwid

Wearing a chocolate fedora

Shouts out

Fleas!

Supernatural Worm!

Better than Homer!

Much better than Homer!

Step up to the stage young man!

Schopenhauer!

Take him through the door

Chain him to the post!

Now

Emperor Tullio reaches over his belly

Fingers a small hip pocket

Pulls out a matchbox

Lights a handy stick

Schopenhauer!

What are you doing?

Schopenhauer!

The chimp's taking off his clothes

It's time to sacrifice Man!

Emperor Tullio shouts

Extending the flaming torch

Expressionless

The chimp blows it out

Drives his right forefinger

Into Tullio's chest

Faster than any Brain can process the Image

Schopenhauer pulls out Tullio's beating heart

And proceeds to slowly eat it

With his bandy legs hanging off the stage

Oblivious

To the shocked crowd turning away

Like the final scene of The Bacchae

Suddenly Everything makes Sense

Now every Monolog every Dialog

Every Image in the Narrative

Shakes the Will-Based Soul

After wiping his bloody hands

On his discarded tunic

Schopenhauer knuckles up

And scampers back to the cave

In the Dolomites

The two lines of Candidates become arcs

Curving towards the Space Art Fair

And the lonely cry of an Irish pennywhistle

Talezen walks dazed through the olive trees

Bumping into twilight spice booths

Circling troupes of street theater

Sculptures that materialize in his path

He has a slice of pumpkin pie

A shot of bourbon

Plays harmonica in a blues band

Around midnight

After performing a new one-line Poem

He's walking home

Thinking hard about the Wicker Man

When he suddenly realizes

Livia vanished

And Metis didn't make it

The Explorers Club

The bright afternoon light
Drifts down through clove
And lingering vanilla
To gild the Welsh oak table
As they enter
And take their big wicker chairs
Kendra
Gwedyllian
Pembrey
And five new Councilors
Who willed the Will
To be Here
The Universe is still in Being
Still generating Space
Talezen begins
We continue to press Time forward
And if the Challenge Metis answered
Was real in all Frames of Reference
Then we can assume

He was victorious

And All is Well

My fellow Councilors

As we await his imminent Return

This Euphoria

This cascading Crest

Will certainly be followed

By deep and treacherous Troughs

So this Moment of Joy

Is the right perfect time

To stand with the Diggers

And create the conditions we describe

We welcome the Talents

Of five new Personalities

Their fresh Energy and Perspective

Will sharpen our syntax

Enhance our vocabulary

We've overcome many fierce

Many sustained Attacks

From Outside and Inside

Many personal Tragedies

And as Rhodri wanted

We're stronger now
We're more vigilant now
We have benign winds in our sails
And no maelstrom in sight
Our Wisdom has been tempered
By the chill of Fire the flames of Ice
We're primed for the Impossible
We're moving on
From the recent disturbing Events
Of disguise and subterfuge
To the launch
Of a major new Project
I've called you here
Under the ancestral sessile Oak
To announce the groundbreaking
Of The Explorers Club
Since the invention of the V Domes
We've relied on the scattered efforts
Of adventurous Individuals
To acquire New Knowledge
Of Deep Space planets
And their biological Intelligence

Today I present a Plan

To discover and name our Successor

On the broad top of Hegel Hill

The Vardons are laying the cornerstone

For a large structure of glass and steel

To house The Explorers Club

Homosapiens to homosagax

Was a fine and fundamental Leap

In the ceaseless work of Self-Creation

But the Sagax Self is just one stop

One station

On that long rocky Road

At some point in the distant Future

We'll need a more powerful

A more durable biological Body

So why wait a thousand

A million years?

In this phase of positive Momentum

Why not test our Advanced Powers

Why not try for the Next Form now?

My fellow Councilors

The Prime Objective

Of the Explorers Club

Is to achieve the Impossible

The Marriage of Sagaxi and Aliens

Yes

Our Body is dependent on oxygen

Dependent on trillions of microbes

Can it survive

A methane atmosphere?

A waterless scorching planet?

A totally different food chain?

Can we develop Voletics technology

To instantaneously transport the Sagax Body

To any destination in The Deep?

Even if we answer these questions

How can we be sure

That interbreeding between Species

Doesn't just produce a race of mules

Hanging around the clubhouse

Complaining about everything

And never producing Progeny?

In Theory

We would want the Alien Form

Different enough

To contribute major genetic advantage

Close enough

To generate erotic attraction

But we must keep our Minds open

To every potential Union

That can further our High Intent

Yes

It could get very interesting

But what's the real probability of success?

Our World is likely just a small bubble

In a mighty sea of Universes

Our understanding of Voletics

Has enabled mental travel

And telepathic communication

But has it altered the Vastness of Space

Or the irrepressible Arrow of Time?

Perhaps

In any case

We need to do more

All our Explorations

Since the founding of the City

Have only scribbled some graffiti
On the Filaments of the Cosmic Web
Even if our Soul Mate
Is Out There waiting for us
Out There looking for us
We don't have the right maps
Or the right orientations
We may not even have the right Minds
To successfully navigate such Immensity
My fellow Councilors
These are starter threads
In a tapestry of Impossibilities
That could potentially block
The consummation of our Desire
Despite these long Odds
When First and Third Wills
Are aligned
With the perfect Goal
We Know
Without knowing
That Everything is Possible
The Passion for our Successor

In the ascending spiral of Life

Will create the Beloved we seek

My Sagaxi

As I was thinking on these things

A clue surfaced

Some time ago

On Byd

Iggy

The Infant God

Took possession of me

Recently

He went away

I think he's disappointed with me

Displeased with Man

I think he's continuing his Education

In another biological Intelligence

Like us

On another planet

Like Earth

If we trace Iggy's recent Motion

If we track him to that Deep Shore

We may find our Will-Based Soul Mate

Far ahead of cosmic schedule

If we need bloodhounds to find this god

Interjects Herve

Then we should release A S I

And ask it to find his smoking trail

Across the impassive Sky

Shouldn't take more than an hour

At quantum computation speeds

Still too dangerous

Talezen replies

We could consult the Eighth Graders

Says Aisling

They have their ways

Still too young

Talezen quickly replies

First contact is critical

Adds Gwendyllian

Our Man will bring slow Courtship

Romantic Style

Pleasing gifts from Earth

We can't be like the boorish Greeks

Seizing foreign women

To compensate for their Need

He'll be handsome

Persuasive

Strong and protective

Our Woman will be clever and exotic

A Seductress who knows

The plants and animals

The herbs and all manner of Healing

An Intellect that can put aside her Vanity

For the Pride of raising the Next Man

She'll be beautiful

Have a fine singing voice

And wear precious jewelry

The Explorers will certainly introduce

Their unique Expressions of Derwid Culture

Says Talezen

Given the importance of this Club

Asks Cerdic

How will the Members be chosen?

By outstanding recent Results

Or High Potential?

By personal Courage and spontaneous Wit

Talezen replies with a smile

My Sagaxi

While considering how best to detect

And follow Iggy's trail

It occurred to me

That he could be emotionally attached

To certain City Personalities

Lawrence Johns was his first teacher

Kendra saved him from the trap

On the Bird Planet

Once we have confirmed

The new configurations of V Domes

And reliable quantum transport

Of the Sagax Body

Anywhere

In the Cosmic Voletic Field

Once the Explorers Club

Is fully enrolled and equipped

I'll ask Kendra

To ask the Infant God

For his current location

And the best routes from Earth

My Sagaxi

Athenapolis was the Impossible Goal

We made it happen

Homosagax was the Impossible Goal

We made it happen

We've come a long way

From Winstanley and St George's Hill

From the Diggers in Haight Ashbury

Now we take Athenapolis to the Stars

To create a Superior Form of Man

Now we take our Will-Based Soul

Beyond the Sagax Self

Now we Fall in Love

Now we Multiply the Mystery

www.ingramcontent.com/pod-product-compliance
Lightning Source LLC
Chambersburg PA
CBHW032223080426
42735CB00008B/688
9781929096190